Managerial
Performance
and Promotability

Managerial Performance and Promotability

The Making of an Executive

MARK B. SILBER
V. CLAYTON SHERMAN

PREFACE

Why do some managers move up the corporate ladder while others are passed by? What makes certain managers unique in their effectiveness? Why do some organizations remain competitive while others stagnate and die? What are the personal characteristics of the manager who succeeds in the real world of organization life? What facilitates leader impact on the organization?

Managerial career progression and effectiveness within an organization are not the impersonal processes that some popular writers would have us believe. They are very personal, very human, and organization-specific. It is an awareness of the interpersonal dynamics and interaction within the organization that assists or impairs managerial career ascent.

We do not attempt here to instruct the men and women in management about what works in their particular world of operation. No one can replace individual perceptions, awareness, and ability to function sensitively. There are no universal truths, no canned formulas for success in this book (nor elsewhere, we suspect). It is in the manager's real organizational world where careers move ahead or founder, where organizations achieve or merely survive. This volume discusses the assumptions and results of the different management styles that characterize various approaches to human interaction with respect to task accomplishment.

All around us can be seen people who are ineffective in their assigned roles, executives failing without knowing they are failing, managers unaware of how to mobilize effectively the human energies in the organization to achieve their business objectives. If a manager is to be effective in the informal organizational world, if his department and organization are to achieve on a continuing basis, he must be able to deal with the human side of managing, with the sometimes irrational aspects of the people with whom he works, their feelings, perceptions, emotional biases, fears, and expectations. It is the manager's situational sensitivity and flexibility that largely determine his success or failure.

The acquisition of managerial power, informal organizational politics, the use and misuse of executive influence, the ethics of corporate living, the real world of career rise and career destruction, effective organization living—these key interests of the management practitioner are the primary focus of this book. We have described what we have observed and experienced as practitioners and consultants and what we have come to believe about managerial and organizational effectiveness and achievement. We have committed to writing our combined years of industrial and organizational experience and have tried to share our perceptions of the realities of management life.

Men often think they are giants without perceiving that they have gained their vantage point by standing on the shoulders of those who have gone before. We acknowledge and are indebted to the work of many outstanding theorists and expert observers. Specific acknowledgment is given to the behavioral scientists who have significantly influenced us—Argyris, Maslow, Herzberg, Vroom, Myers, Levinson, Gellerman, Feinberg, Drucker, Allen, MacGregor, Guion, Blake, Shartle, Reddin, and others—whose insights and key points regarding managerial effectiveness have become part of the generally accepted body of modern managerial practice and understanding. We have attempted to build on these insights, and on the basis of our own experiential understanding, to interpret them to today's manager.

We have followed the advice of our editors in using male pronouns throughout the text rather than the awkward juxtapositions of he and she, him and her. By this generic usage we mean to include and refer to all leaders and managers, both male and female.

We would also like to express our personal appreciation to our families, our college professors and mentors, and the many industrial executives under and with whom we have learned. Their care and concern, their tough-minded influence, and their high standards, toward whose achievement we stretched ourselves, assisted in forming this work.

MARK B. SILBER
V. CLAYTON SHERMAN

CONTENTS

PART ONE

ORGANIZATION BEHAVIOR

If anything can go wrong, it will.

Nothing is as easy as it looks.

Everything takes longer than you think it will.

—*Murphy's Laws*

An Inside Look at the Informal World

Organization life is a world of tension in which the manager cannot be fully independent as he seeks to meet his accountabilities. This tension is the result of conflicts between what he wants to do and the way the business requires that he respond.

Many managers feel they are tied down by policies, practices, and procedures. But industry is built on and runs on an unstructured world of informal relationships, and the manager's environment is not quite as structured as it appears on the surface. The organization is a highly fluid environment—free-floating and amorphous—and thus sometimes difficult to comprehend. Relationships are continually changing. Often an action that the manager takes can be like hitting a bag filled with water: the bag may give in one place while the water spurts out in another.

THE PAYOFF MATRIX

Dr. Gene Booker illustrates the informal world of the organization by presenting an image where different lengths of yarn are strung from the ceiling to the floor and to the four walls until an entire room is filled with intersecting and connecting lines. These pieces of yarn, or vectors, represent power influence and interpersonal impacts. To complicate it even further, some of these pieces of yarn are of different lengths and some have offshoots; others have weights attached to them. Still further, and to fully represent the complexity of the informal world, every other month or so change the various weights on the different lines, string new lines, and remove old ones.

This complicated set of interrelationships illustrates that the impact of the work you, the manager, do at any given point in time in the informal world is directly tied to the influence and power of others. And since their power and influence vary with time, the payoff for the effort you expend is constantly changing. Furthermore, the assignments that are important to your boss today may not be important to him two weeks from now. Thus the extrinsic value of the work you do is constantly changing. And what has high return for your career in terms of visibility and political sponsorship is tied to, but is also separate from, the value of the work done itself.

This suggests a dynamic state. Incorrect information about the relevant status of various situations in your own informal world will be amplified in your career. Thus it is important to be tuned in to the informal world and tuned in to your executive and his changing expectations. Do not assume that your job description is in any way complete or even accurate. If you believe that your job can be defined on paper or that the stated duties are your only assignments, then you are organizationally naive. In fact, your position accountabilities are constantly being updated by your executive. Like a baseball player, you do not play in the same game day in and day out.

Because values and anticipations change, it is important to understand that working on projects or tasks that are no longer valued by management is meaningless work. True, completing work gives one a feeling of accomplishment, but to stick to a task simply because it is intrinsically difficult or because it is interesting is not the strategy that produces winning players. What wins the ball game in the informal world is knowing what is important today, and what assignments and projects will pay off today and tomorrow.

We are not in favor of the conforming yes-man, who always wants to do the will of his boss or who feels that the boss is all-important. What we are suggesting is that it is important for you to focus on those things that produce payoff—for both you and your company. If you are uncomfortable starting and stopping, if you are full of anxiety when the boss says, "That's right, you were working on that assignment, but it's not quite as important now as this one," then you ought to take a look at yourself. These constantly changing needs of management are a reality of the organization world. The ability to give up work or to stop participating in a project, and the courage to coordinate your thinking with that of your executive, are necessary for your career progress and are vital to the continued growth of your company.

CHANGING RELATIONSHIPS

One of our traditional notions about our interpersonal relationships has been that we will have our friends forever. The building of working relationships in the informal world requires us repeatedly to form close friendships with people in the organization. However, to fantasize that these will continue through time is a delusion. As you change locations within a company, horizontally or vertically, you may want to examine some of the relationships that you are maintaining. You should remember that you have only 24 hours a day, only one weekend every week. The question is, how are you going to allocate that time?

It's Not What You Know . . .

We are suggesting that organization associations change over time. There is some truth to the notion that associating with the right people will help you get ideas through the system and see changes implemented. The informal world of organization life is one of influence, power, flexible trade-offs, and negotiation. If you think for one minute that your ideas get through the system because they are right, they are the best, they are the only way to fly, then you are living in a fantasy world. Things happen in any organization structure because of negotiations, trade-offs, selling, and a continuing succession of informal coalitions.

It is certainly true that the need for power leverage among agents of change within the organization—sponsors or the "right" associates, those who have sufficiently more clout or a specialized influence that managers can draw upon to get things done in the system—is valid. Not only is their sponsorship necessary for getting things to happen in the organization, it is also essential to managers in terms of career growth.

Nevertheless, it has been pointed out by managers that one doesn't necessarily have to go through the system to get results. There are numerous roles to be played in the group dynamics of the informal world, among them the problem solver, the clown, the informal leader, the peacemaker, the nonconformist, and the person who rattles the cage of anyone who's sitting around the table.

If you don't want to fit within the system, but prefer to fight it and revolutionize the world about you, then you can play the role of nonconformist. It is a role that is played with self-satisfaction, and it can be fulfilling if you can act as a catalyst for your group and get them to think differently and to reevaluate their own assumptions. But if you choose this role of restive nonconformity, then you must know that there are positive and negative consequences attached to it, as there are to all roles. The role of the iconoclast is not played to win popularity contests, and if you adopt it you must be willing to pay the consequences.

Personal Friendships

When we assume a new role we find, sometimes, that we are eliminating old acquaintances from our association patterns. This does not mean that we sacrifice friendship on the altar of politics, but there seems to be an evolving pattern of associating with the right people at different times. The topic is usually avoided in the textbooks because it is an area that is highly value-loaded. We have observed that when a man is promoted from supervisor to departmental manager, the old patterns of whom he rides with in the car pool, whether he continues to ride in a car pool at all, whom he associates with during luncheon breaks, and whom he plays cards or golf with, all seem to bear a relationship to his new position within the hierarchy. His association patterns both on and off the job tend to change. We are not saying that this is the right way to behave or that it is the only way to behave, but we have seen it happen with many managers as they change their position within the organization.

One of the most difficult people to impress this reality upon will be your wife, because she has been associating with Mary Smith, whose husband has been a fellow supervisor with you, for years. Now that you have the promotion and he doesn't, do you still associate as frequently with the Smiths? This will be a personal choice on your part. As you move up into successive slots within the organization, probably you will begin to emphasize other associations and contacts. This will happen because there are other people in the informal world with whom you need to share values. Associations are established in the informal world partly because you need the insights of certain people; you need their values or their information in order to be fully effective in your own position. These evolving relationships are necessary if you are to cultivate political contacts and sponsorship to get your ideas through the system.

Tuning In to Changing Power

Being aware in the informal world is being aware of the changing sub rosa relationships, the person-to-person sensitivities, the informal political values and taboos, and the informal understandings between functions and among people within the functions, as well as knowing what thou shalt and shalt not do. Arrangements within this unstructured world are seldom written down; there are no descriptions of the informal interpersonal credit bank—in fact, the entire power dimension is never fully described. You must gain your awareness by tuning in to the arrangement to sense who has the clout, power, influence, direction.

Many people find it difficult to live in this informal world. They like to have things spelled out neatly. They believe that if you want to get something done you must go through the system, rigidly following its procedures and practices. We are not being radical, nor are we suggesting organizational disobedience by any stretch of the imagination. Naturally the system should be used when it serves your purposes. But if something has to be accomplished rapidly because there is political or informal pressure to get it done, then the man who succeeds is the man who knows the informal arrangements and makes use of his contacts.

Some managers go about establishing informal relationships ineptly, inappropriately, and in a dependent, ingratiating manner. Their efforts backfire. If they are unable emotionally to understand the system, they are cut out of it; they have died in terms of organization life. The undeniable reality is that people in management live in a world where the relationships of power and influence are constantly changing.

If you are tuned in to this world, you know who was in power last month. You know who is going to be promoted in a particular area. You are aware of who has the contacts, who's the informal Richelieu behind the throne, the man to see to get something done. You also know that a particular person has fallen from favor and that he is no longer influential or effective. In fact, knowing who is in and who can make things happen is basic to success in the informal world.

We recently heard of a change at the top levels of a particular hierarchy. The announcement of the change was couched in very formal language, filled with regrets, and had all the earmarks of "we're protecting the organization." Those who knew this specific informal world knew why the person left the payroll: a power inversion occurred, and even though he once was part of a powerful political bloc, this man lost out. The problem was that he had too rigidly aligned himself in a political, collaborative relationship within an arena of shifting power.

Coalitions and trade-offs within the informal world are constantly changing. Charlie, George, Mary, and you may collaborate to get something accomplished with your boss. For all intents and purposes, that coalition is over when the goal is reached. If you think that Charlie will forever maintain the collaborative power relationship with you, you are mistaken. Just as there is political appreciation vertically within the hierarchy, there is also political appreciation laterally between peers, but it is dynamic in content and context through time.

Some people are failing in their careers and do not know why. They cannot understand why they are ineffective, because they have done everything according to the book. Yet the book is not everything. If a manager is blind to this dynamic environment, then it will catch him short, punish him, and eventually decrease his effectiveness. Some people have difficulty in living with the ambiguity and the anxiety that it creates; others cannot live with it at all. They are unable to deal with the intrigue and the importance of keeping their senses tuned in to who is in power and how things are done in the organization world.

The self-evaluation question that every man in management should ask himself is whether he is comfortable in such a situation. If the answer is no, perhaps life in the large-scale organization is not for him. And he should feel no shame in not being able to deal with the mind bending that occurs in organization life. There is yet time for him to become the maharajah of his own firm.

Staying Flexible

In all group living there is a jockeying for position, a need to define one's role in relation to the other people at the conference table. There are also needs for self-expression, visibility, and idea influence. Yet these competitive feelings operate at variance with the group norm that says we all have to hang together, that we all have to play on the same team for greater effectiveness in task accomplishment, and that we are here for mutual problem solving—and no one must be himself at the expense of the group. So managers are caught in the dilemma of playing a self-centered role and playing the role of the nice guy.

It is extremely important to be flexible in this continuum, to know when to use the power you have and when not to use it, when to admit your dependence and when to show independence. Both the manager who is always dependent and the one who is constantly using his muscle lose. Agility is needed in organization life, and uncertainty over when to show power and dependence creates managerial tension.

Dependence and Independence

In the informal world, often people don't know when they should demonstrate strength, although they usually know when to be conforming. Some people feel that the way to get through job life is to be weak, dependent, and always accepting. Many men live out their careers according to this behavior model. The organizational dishrag or clinging vine recalls the mentality of the Southern belle. There are a lot of Southern belles in organizations. But adopting such an attitude is a manipulative technique to gain self-centered ends. And it is important managerially to recognize this passive hostility as a way of controlling and dominating others.

On the other hand, some people consider every situation a Mount Everest to be scaled. They continually feel the need to conquer, to charge up and win another victory. These people have difficulty in asking for help. They never want to be dependent because they regard an offensive position as an expression of their mastery. For these people there is never room for an honest "I don't know. I could use some help on this."

The interesting thing is that both these behavior models operate within each of us to varying degrees. We all tend to vacillate between the emotional poles of dependence and independence. We all wonder when to back down, to defer, and when to ask for assistance and to be interdependent with others. Knowing the answers is a valuable secret of leadership and flexibility in leadership. It is also a key insight for being an effective subordinate.

During our confusing years of adolescence, we thought we wanted to be fully independent, to be a "man's man." But it is not unusual to find a manager who is afraid to show his power and the strength of his independent convictions. He says to himself, "I'm director of this big function, but now that I have the power I don't know how or when to exercise it." At the other extreme is the manager who immediately assumes the emperor's crown the first time he is able to sign his name on the company forms. He says to himself, "Today the division, tomorrow the world. I'm on the way up; get out of my way. I've got power."

In both cases, the managers are reacting inappropriately to the power that is given to them. Exercise of power does not mean that you ring the button, have the troops sent in, and stand them at attention. Power is exercised when you say no or I'm sorry. Power is when you can influence your boss with a new idea or defend a subordinate from attack. It's telling someone to get things moving so that a job can be done. To exercise power effectively and with a sense of ethics is an indication of strength and courage.

There will be times when you realize that you have power in your organization. You have all the formal and informal clout that is necessary to make things happen. But you also realize that if you pull the plug in the bathtub to change a situation, you may run the risk of being the one who goes down the drain. There will be times when you do not use the formal authority you have, when you will have the ace but will not play it. The manager who plays his ace every time may very well lose in the overall organization card game. The way to win is to watch the executives around you who are successful in achieving goals. *Notice how they use power.* Notice how they show their dependence and when they show independence.

Committeeism

One interesting aspect of organization life, one that requires interdependent interaction with others, is the phenomenon of committeeism. We seem to live more and more with joint decision-making processes. In some cases, the reason may be that individuals refuse to take a stand, to be independent, to relish high-risk, high-reward relationships; or perhaps it is just their self-doubt and inability to believe fully in their own ideas. Or it may be that joint decision making is a consequence of the interdependence of functions in highly complex and organized structures. Whatever the genesis of this diffused decision making, people adapting to the decision-making role have to deal with the conflict of expressing their own individuality while living together with others.

The source of the stress in committee behavior is the inherent conflict between the individual's wanting to look good and to stand out in an aggressive fashion, to seize the leadership of the process, on the one hand, and, on the other, his desire to be accepted and belong to the group, hoping that others see him as a facilitator and a necessary member of that group. The secret of how to manage this source of tension is to be *inoffensively compatible* and at the same time to express your own ideas in terms of making something happen.

The skillful manager learns to fit in, to be helpful and supportive, and to give consultation freely in the group relationship. Power in leadership must be used gently in order to maintain inoffensive compatibility. This does not mean that you blend in with everyone else or that you give up your best ideas and your ethics; but it does suggest the importance of openly listening to what other people in the group are saying. It is important to recognize that you are there to be *problem* centered rather than *self* centered.

So what is called for is control of self-presentation. Observation shows that the people who become leaders in informal groups—those who emerge as men to whom others look for direction, values, and guidance—somehow carry off this presentation of themselves and their ideas in an inoffensively compatible fashion.

WINNING

To be effective in the informal world, as well as to further your career, it is important to recognize that achievement is ultimately built on a series of short gains. One of the hard realities of the group decision-making process that characterizes organization life is that there are very few total victories. In other words, you must be willing to negotiate so that you can accomplish again. Rather than going for the promised land on your first thrust, be willing to accommodate by growing through a lesser position.

One of the most inane statements seen on any executive's wall goes something like this: "A partial victory is a total defeat." If this is his basic assumption, you can imagine the punishing consequences of some ramifications of his behavior. Perhaps that explains why he has been fired from three different companies in seven years.

Our managerial assumptions determine our behavior, and you must face the reality that, in general, you can hope to achieve only a series of short gains, vital thrusts, short-term payoffs, and coalition victories in a relevant time span. One way to gauge your effectiveness is to review the number of decisions you have asked for and see whether you have had more advances than defeats. Some people get themselves into a win-lose situation because they shoot for all or nothing. If you choose to go for total victory, if you insist on making the other person all wrong, if you desire to vindicate your position totally, then by all means realize that your attitude will have its consequences.

Timing

The informal world is not all black and white. It is a gray world of many subtleties. If you compare the "troublemaker" and the "brainchild," you may notice one factor that distinguishes them: their sensitivity in knowing when to introduce change. The employee who doesn't fly with other people, who is annoying and perceived as a troublemaker, creates noise in the system. He just doesn't know when to make his ideas for change known.

Think back to the last time you failed to get something accepted. Think about the last time you were unsuccessful in introducing something. Or the time when you were made aware that your disappearance from the company wouldn't make much difference. Now think about the time when you were seen as the fair-haired boy, the one who seemed automatically to be able to implement his ideas for change effectively. The crucial difference was that you knew when to introduce the changes, how to introduce them, how hard to nudge or push when you introduced them, and whether they hit your boss's central values. The subtlety is in timing, in knowing who should assist, and in realizing that none of this is spelled out and that you must rely on your organizational finesse and interpersonal credit-bank assets.

VALUES IN THE INFORMAL WORLD

Many values govern the relationships of managers in organization life. Some of these values are explicit, the stated values of the world of business. Other values are unstated but are endorsed by the group because they are necessary to the smooth functioning of the informal world. It is important to tune in to and be guided by these mores even more closely than by the explicit values of industry. Although values in the informal world vary by organization and by the group of people you work with, some are common to most organizations.

Waste Treatment

Organizational environments are quite explicit in emphasizing, for example, full utilization of time, people, and materials. The constant theme is high utility, low waste. Efficiency is one of the prime values in America, along with bigness, speed, and power. It is also one of the official values of the formal world of industry. Conversely, the informal world condones occasional goofing off and acknowledges the right to spend time building relationships on company time, even if this means low utilization of manpower minutes.

It is our recommendation that you invest in some "low-efficiency" human interaction. On the surface, the informal meetings at the water cooler or at the secretary's desk, the extra-long coffee breaks, the 15-minute conversations may appear to be a waste of time, and how much of this you as a manager can tolerate depends on your own anxiety as well as on what your group is actually producing. But to discount that time as wasted is shortsightedness, because during that time informal relationships are being built, political arrangements are being made, and people are indirectly trying to get things through the system. Employees are psychologically stroking each other, making the office "a good place to work." People use this wasted time to evolve certainty out of organization uncertainty. Let's face it: Your behavior in supervision will create some uncertainty. Your employees are going to have difficulty living with your ambiguity at times. While it may look as if employees are boondoggling, they may in fact be accomplishing things that will help them be effective in their jobs and help you look good.

Thus there is value in going through a time-investment process. It produces power in relationships, and those relationships in turn facilitate getting something done. So the five minutes of down time and wasted time on the phone or at coffee is likely to put something through the informal system or even the formal system for you.

Other Guidelines in the Informal World

Pay your debts. When you find yourself in a coalition or a dependent relationship and you owe a reciprocal favor, recognize that you must repay that informal, but real, debt. If you welsh on your return understandings in the informal world, you will be ostracized and your reputation will suffer.

Honor your word. When you make an arrangement in the informal world, keep it. If you commit yourself to a political position in a joint venture, then ride with it. You must never let the person who takes the leadership in presenting your combined new idea or suggestion for change stand alone. When he, as a change agent, makes the introduction you must be with him. If you make commitment noises, then you must follow through.

Stay conscious of return on investment. One of your obligations is to your company's financial well-being. Your company exists to make a profit, and therefore your job and other people's jobs depend on the ability of "our" company to make a profit. Yet many managers have little real awareness of the contribution they need to make for ROI. Profit to them is an intellectual concept. They have their expense accounts and their conventions to go to and they use the duplicating machine as if it had no cost. Somehow they have the feeling that the company owes all cost-generating benefits to them. They see the company as a big benefit dispenser. However, the inherent charge of management is that of stewardship, trusteeship. If the terms "trustee" and "steward" are only words to you, then chances are that you will labor in your career progress. If you don't sincerely feel the criticality of those words, you may be only playing games and roles in management.

Adhere to policies. Policies are written for intent and guidance. They are not there to be beaten or gotten around or ignored. The man who joins management identifies with management. The person who survives in the formal and informal worlds is the person who identifies with policies—not because he is a robot, but because he appreciates that policies are there for an interdependent reason. This does not mean that antiquated policies should not be abandoned or that there aren't better ways of doing things. It simply means that the manager has an informal and formal obligation to support the policy positions of his own company.

If you function in a union setting, then you should realize that the union contract is as sacred as any other contract. If you are coy with the union contract, then you are guilty of organization adultery. That contract is to be honored, not voided, by your behavior. You have an obligation to the people in the bargaining unit and you have an obligation to the informal world of your fellow managers who are trying to live by the contract. It is important that you honor not only the letter of the contract but its intent. To manipulate the contract, to try to circumvent it, only brings retribution—in the formal grievance process as well as with your peers in the informal managerial world.

ASSUME THE ROLE OF MANAGER

Command of Yourself

Through this aura of confusion, through this dizzying uncertainty and constant change in terms of whom to contact and how to get things done, we have observed that the man who moves ahead not only knows the informal world and stays tuned in to it, but carries himself with confidence and optimism. Much of what he sees may turn his stomach. He may inflict self-torture upon himself through an executive ulcer or mental unrest. But the day he shows this discomfort, this lack of self-assuredness, he will find that no one is going to rescue him and that the organizational birds of prey will gather to watch the wounded animal. You must learn to control and discipline your emotions and always be in command of yourself. You must be able to carry within yourself the uneasiness that we all have from time to time.

People are concerned about their inadequacies; they are concerned about the possibility of failing and of being less than what other people expect of them. All we can say is that you are part of the human race. The question is how to handle stress and live with it. The time and place for letting it all hang out is not, unfortunately, during work conflict and crisis.

Emotionality Versus Rationality:
Yours and That of Your Subordinates

At the very heart of the manager's job are the tensions he must deal with, tensions not only within himself, but within the group whose dynamics he is asked to manage. Above and beyond being able to bear the load that organization life imposes goes the managerial ability to carry oneself with the optimism and confidence that shows personal strength. One of the values that we hold in terms of organization life is that a manager should be thoughtful and introspective. Companies expect that a man in organization life will not show the emotional side of his makeup. He is supposed to be analytical, rational, even-tempered, never hot-headed, and he is expected to possess all the "manly" traits that our society values.

To a certain extent the face you show as a manager reflects the reality of your particular organization and is essential to your personal and leadership success. But the full reality is that you are a feeling human being first and a manager second. Because you are a human being, you know that people are emotional and that things are not always done on the basis of cold hard facts or reason. Many decisions, fortunately or unfortunately, are made on an emotional, a judgmental, or an experiential basis. This life-history mass, this pulling together from all our past experiences and our present perceptions and prejudices and feelings, has a direct impact on the decision-making process. And yet, when a person lets his emotions show through, when he expresses his discomfort, frustration, or anger, the system tends to punish him for that behavior. The kiss of death in American industry is the label "emotionally unstable."

Sometimes the bully or the cantankerous person, the employee you can hear through the office walls and down the hallway as he blusters and bluffs his way through organization life, overwhelms the opposition. But eventually the system punishes him and his acceptability diminishes over time. Many people who have gained prominence and power through knowledge have turned that power to dictatorial rule. But such highly individualistic expression tends to be discounted, and eventually the system stops tolerating it.

At the same time that we recognize the need for skill in expressing our ideas, we also affirm that it is important to let people know how we feel. The question is, *how* do you let them know? You don't have to come unglued and spill over on people in order to get the message across that you are frustrated. The opposite—tying yourself into knots by holding in your frustration—is not the answer either. No job is worth the psychosomatic disorders commonly seen among people in organization life: the gastritis, the palm sweating, the insomnia, the nervous ticks. Neither is there a job worth six months in a mental institution. One of the secrets of dealing with the informal world is knowing how to present yourself as rational, logical, and analytical, and, at the same time, presenting yourself as a fully functioning human being and dealing adequately with the emotional component.

It is important to be sensitive to the environment in which you work. How do the executives act? How do they dress? How do they talk to each other? How open are they? Different organizations reinforce different behaviors. Some companies, for example, politically reinforce no smoking at all, and others say you are really not with it unless you smoke a pipe. Some organizations admit that theirs is a rough ball game. They welcome you into the jungle. If you survive, fine, but you are indirectly warned that you are expected to play to win in a punishing environment. On the other hand, they may not care if you walk in barefoot with your hair down to your bunions as long as you produce.

A lot of this is superficial, but your environment, superficial or not, is important to you. What we suggest is that you tune in to those work-climate values that are accepted and reinforced in your own environment and be aware of what is not tolerated. If you are highly emotional and you really need to let go occasionally, then you should make sure that you are in the kind of environment that tolerates this behavior. If people in your organization are low on self-trust and interpersonal trust, and if this atmosphere doesn't fit your set of values, then perhaps you should get out of that overcontrolled microsociety.

It should be recognized that there are some work environments where people are so beaten down that they withdraw from any kind of emotional expression. Unfortunately, there are far too many ambulatory basket cases in organizations. These people are living isolates, guarded and passive. They have emotionally withdrawn from trustful interaction; their decision is not to make a decision. They are neither for people nor against people, neither for production nor against production; organizationally, they are merely existing and using the cafeteria. Some have chosen this behavior as their mode of adjustment in order to exist, whereas others may see it as the only way to survive. Each of us has to decide how he wants to live and where he can function effectively.

We encourage organizations to understand and promote interpersonal sensitivity. Employees should be recognized as human beings and should be allowed to show their individuality. The manager has a quasi-psychotherapeutic role in letting his people get their tensions off their chest. He can establish a minienvironment within his organization where people can express themselves and where he can give emotional support and encouragement to them during difficult periods. Of course, he should also express his negative feelings when his staff works poorly. He must be able to tell a man when he has done poorly and let his disappointment show. The manager who is able to deal effectively with this conflict between emotionality and rationality is aware that when he hires someone, he is buying not only the mountain peaks but also some valleys. And so he uses his managerial judgment to determine when to be manifestly concerned over marginal performance and when to encourage and lend support to the developing employee.

Father Time

One of the concerns we hear repeatedly from managers is how best to use their time. Time is the only resource that everyone has in equal quantities: 24 hours a day. But while you are reading this book, for example, making an effort toward development, some of your peers are watching television. Managerial concern about the allocation of time is a source of frustration and tension. The manager is charged with long-range planning efforts, and at the same time he has to put out the brushfire problems. He is charged with leading his group through an organized plan but is constantly faced with variances from the plan. The many distractions he must deal with often make him despair.

What can you do to manage your time better? First of all, confront yourself; recognize that some things need to be let go and that, as a manager, you have responsibility and authority to determine what those things might be. If the efforts you are expending on a particular project are not making a significant contribution, then abandon that project. Confront your boss, who might have given you that job two months ago, and suggest that the project is no longer useful. Confront the people who are still calling meetings, still initiating memos, and adding nothing. You may just find that reducing the amount of unnecessary effort reduces tension all down the line.

The Doer and the Facilitator

Management specialists are highly cognizant of the importance of functioning in their own role rather than doing the job of their employees. They recognize that they are no longer the doers but the managers. It seems strange to think of a manager as being other than a doer. But he is a pro at managing an area or a task force. He is a pro at getting something through the system. He hires other people to be the problem solvers and is no longer a problem solver himself.

Your role as a manager is to help the group solve its problems. You are there to see that the problems are identified, handled, and solved, and that the solutions are controlled. You are there to provide support, to let other people bounce ideas off you as they create alternative solutions to their problems, and to make a firm decision between alternatives. But you are not there to solve the problems.

In this same vein, you are no longer the oracle of good answers. Instead, you focus on *asking good questions*. The people who work with you should have the good answers, the reliable information, the valid viewpoints. They stimulate you and provide you with action-oriented answers. Your responsibility is to ask the right questions of the right people at the right time and to get the information in the right form.

The informal world is a world of tension and ambiguity. The effective manager is the one who tunes in to the subtleties of this environment and facilitates the informal relationships that allow others to get the job done.

2

Why Do People
Behave as They Do?

Why is human behavior so complex? Why is it so difficult to predict what an employee will do? Why can't we expect total commitment from those who work with us? What makes an employee do or not do a specific action? Why don't people always behave as they should?

In this chapter we discuss a few of the variables in the psychological mix of behavior. No doubt, you will come to the conclusion that predicting behavior is difficult, whether it is the behavior of your fellow executives, your boss, or your staff.

WHAT MAKES SAMMY RUN?

The origins of behavior are diverse. Behavior is determined by a number of psycho-socio-situational variables whose interaction may be additive, multiplicative, or even suppressive. There is a kind of formula that allows us to predict how variables interact as people move through their job lives and how they affect job behavior. Although we do not know the precise impact of these variables on behavior or on each other, we can identify some of them and show how they make people behave as they do.

Some of these variables, or factors, are

- Past experience
- Needs
- Abilities and talents
- Self-image
- Ethics and morality
- Motivation
- Situation opportunity
- Risk orientation
- Perception of authority
- Management by objectives

These variables interact to form behavior patterns, and while other variables may be involved here we shall deal only with these major factors. The order of these components is unimportant; each will have different, highly personalized weights in different situations. Each component interacts within different people in a different manner, at different levels of consciousness, at different times, and with different intensities. These variances seem to relate to the way a particular individual perceives a specific situation or person and the emotional significance of that situation to him. They are the components that determine whether an employee pulls with or against his supervisor.

Although this presentation is simplified and is hardly adequate to describe the complexity of any specific situation, it does highlight certain dimensions of behavior and points to important areas for discussion. Knowing how these variables operate will not enable you to predict behavior with total accuracy, but it will enhance your understanding of why people behave the way they do.

No doubt for some readers the generality of this discussion raises anxiety. But we are dealing with an approximation of a behavior model. It is not exact, but neither is it happenstance. It would be easier if we could pontificate or prophesy. However, we want to suggest that your performance as a manager is a result of many variables, just as the responses of the individuals with whom you interact are made up of complex emotional and social factors.

Although organization life is highly complex and variable, as opposed to being static and highly predictable, we can rely on the tendency for human behavior to repeat itself. As a manager you should be able to discern behavior patterns in your subordinates over time.

PAST EXPERIENCE

The influence of past experience on behavior is self-evident. We are living examples, or results, of multiple influences that have occurred in our lives. The way we integrate our past with our present produces many of the attitudes, perceptions, and values that determine how we behave now as well as how we shall face the future.

Think of all the ways in which your past experience differs from that of a fellow executive. You probably come from a different religious and social background. He may come from a wealthy family and you from a middle-class family. He may have traveled widely; you may think a visit to a neighboring city is a big trip. Some of your employees may be "night" people; others may think the world stops at 5 o'clock. Some may come from families of professionals; others may come from immigrant families.

Past experiences and exposures even affect time orientation. Some people are "now" people. Some, at age 32, are already talking about the good old days or what might have been. Others are future oriented— building a pier for when their ship comes in. Some employees will base their behavior on "if" situations. Still others will agonize over past decisions, while some can integrate very quickly into a present situation.

One's life experiences determine how a person will make decisions and assumptions, the kinds of risks he will take, and the orientation he has toward self and others.

Since much of our present orientation is based on the past, it is important for you to understand the past experiences of your boss. You have to be sensitive to his values and biases, and make your presentations to him through his past orientation. If you don't, your suggestions will go nowhere. The key is to intertwine yourself into his value system and to gain an understanding of his past experiences. This doesn't mean that you must adopt his values for your own, but you must understand them in order to relate to them.

Every one of us has skeletons in our psychological closet. They represent some part of our life that was sensitized, some area in which we were ineffective or where our actions resulted in an emotionally painful experience. Because of such experience, some people are scarred for life. Others have the resiliency to bounce back from those pains, frustrations, and disappointments and go on to function adequately. We are significantly influenced by what happened in our past, but we need not be chained by our yesterdays.

The Leadership Setting

It is important to realize that each person who works for you comes from a different experience background, and it is through their past experiences that people perceive positively or negatively what you ask of them. For some, a request will be seen as a threat because in similar situations they have had disappointment and failure. Others will seize upon the same request with great gusto because a similar past experience has been associated with positive rewards and satisfactions. Therefore, every time you direct your subordinates in a task or make a request of your boss, appreciate that their perception will be colored by their own personal experiences.

One key to management success is to avoid putting someone on the defensive and arousing hostility. Nobody wants to be reminded of his shortcomings or have his fears brought to the surface. Because any request carries with it the possibility of raising old skeletons, you must first think through how your request may be interpreted. You should be aware of people's tender areas, where they have been hurt and where they might have been frustrated. Because of your consideration for other human beings, you will not play on their psychological Achilles' heel. You must be a human being first, a manager second.

F Reactions

As you approach a person—whether it be a subordinate or your boss—remember that what may not seem difficult to you may seem insurmountably difficult to someone else. Try to understand his perceptual world and past experiences by learning about them and being sensitive to them. Then make your request or present your idea on the basis of this knowledge. This can be done only by getting to know your people. While that sounds like a cliché, in this context it is sound. If you are to be an effective manager, you must know where your subordinates are strong and where they are weak. You must also know how they perceive themselves.

Handing out job assignments insensitively produces F reactions: fight, fright, flight, faking, self-flagellation, and emotional fatigue. You can expect these reactions when a man cannot adjust to others' demands. If an assignment or request doesn't match his own perception of success, or if his anticipation of the consequences is negative, he will fight you or try to escape from you, or he will be immobilized with fear and become self-punishing or deceitful. He may react with emotional fatigue. If you get such reactions, you should ask yourself where you are being insensitive to people's past experiences.

THE NEEDS HIERARCHY

Abraham Maslow is renowned for his clarification of the needs that affect human motivation. The management literature has long maintained that the primary factors affecting motivation are those that move us toward satisfaction of our various needs. Because of their relevance we will discuss those needs briefly.

Maslow's classic illustration diagrammed the five areas of need as a hierarchy, with the levels rising from physiological at the base to self-actualization at the apex.

Physiological Needs

Physiological (or biological) needs are the basic human needs. The needs for food, sleep, space, and a basic sense of homeostatic well-being are potent motivators. In a serious recession with high unemployment rates, people are usually content to stay in their jobs, maintaining the status quo, because the need to survive is, *at that time,* their prime motivation. As Dr. Maslow said, people do live by bread alone when there is no bread. Throughout our lives this need area remains one of the strongest.

Security Needs

The next level of needs is security—security from arbitrary, unilateral treatment, from being on the short end of the stick without having any control of our own destiny. Certainly in a working environment, to be subject to the boss's whims can make a person feel very uncomfortable. Assuming that the physiological needs are met, in such a situation you will no doubt look for another boss, one who can relate to you more positively.

A facet of the security need area is consistency in relationships. Employees must be able to predict what will happen in their job environment and how their boss will react in a particular situation.

Social Needs

The third level is the need for acceptance. This area encompasses our need for love, understanding, and belonging. In a working environment it is vital to feel that you belong and that your contribution is important. If you are made to feel that your job is unimportant, or if the group shuts you out of the coffee hour conversations or the friendly repartee, your performance motivation will be impaired.

Esteem Needs

Once a person has been accepted by the group, his need for self-esteem emerges. Not only is it important for us to be accepted socially, but we must feel important as well. Our concern here is job-centered since much of our self-image is associated with the kind of work we do. Ask yourself the following question: Is my work important? Is there anything about my tasks that makes me feel important? Am I giving my time to something that enhances my self-respect?

Self-Actualization Needs

Dr. Maslow noted that once the lower level needs are satisfied they no longer motivate; that is, a satisfied need is not a motivator, and no additional benefit in that area will motivate to any great extent. Thus corporate managers must look to the higher levels of the pyramid for additional motivation release.

At the apex of the pyramid is self-actualization or personal fulfillment. This need includes not only feeling important but also feeling that you are doing your best and becoming everything you are capable of being. In a sense, it is the feeling that you have met and mastered yourself, that you have become involved in your job as a fully functioning human being. This need is an extremely powerful motivator.

The Needs Hierarchy in Business

As we look at Maslow's needs-motivation model, we can see its direct application to organization life. Companies began to minister to the physical-level needs of their employees with the passage of child labor laws and the emergence in the 1920s of the powerful labor unions. Labor and government pressures brought about the fringe benefits designed to take care of many of the security needs. This was the era when Social Security was introduced, and more and more companies began to see the value of satisfying people's needs for life, health, and retirement insurance as a way to reduce anxiety and to heighten motivation.

With most of their basic needs fulfilled, employees are now moving toward the higher levels of the hierarchy. Today there is a fantastic amount of turnover in industry, with great migration from company to company. Loyalty to a particular corporation is no longer considered as important as loyalty to one's own fulfillment. Management is being sorely challenged to satisfy employee higher-level needs and to produce the required return on investment for the company and the return on self-investment for the employee. Job enrichment to liven the deadening effects of production-line work is being demanded, and joint decision-making committees with management are being postulated as employees seek ways to innovate and change their work environment.

Unsatisfied lower-level needs make it difficult to stimulate anyone by filling a higher-level need. It is foolish to talk to a hungry person about self-actualization. As a supervisor, you must help fulfill employee lower-level needs before you can appeal to the higher levels. Conversely, when an employee is ready to function at a higher level, forcing him to remain at a lower level is insensitive and wasteful. It is important to know how to manage people at the level of their existing needs. Discovering where an employee is in his own learning process, knowledge, and self-fulfillment will enable a manager to know what motivates, and what is important to, the employee.

We deal with a person at the level of his need not only because we are seeking happiness for him, but because we are looking for motivation release in job performance. It is doubtful whether any correlation exists between being happy on the job and being productive. Many unhappy people are highly productive, and some who are extremely happy on the job will not or cannot produce adequately. The main principle is to lead people from their present assignments by way of their needs to assignments at a level relevant to those needs. Individual employees should be treated uniquely, in line with their specific personal circumstances.

ABILITIES AND TALENTS

Our needs are the prime releasing and motivating forces in our job lives that move us toward the things we want to do. Our abilities constitute the essential factor that determines what we can do. Abilities are composites of the knowledge and skills we have acquired, as well as the native talents we bring to the job. Unfortunately, many people are afraid to do a particular job because they think it calls for knowledge beyond that which they have. Frequently, however, such self-limitations are mythical. Conversely, some employees have an inflated concept of their abilities.

One key to successful management is the ability to identify people's individual skills, to know what your employees are truly capable of doing. The discovery of certain limitations in an employee is not cause for ridicule or chastisement. It is an opportunity to increase your own knowledge of what skills you have to work with in terms of that particular person. Our point is that the supervisor should focus on working with people in their areas of competence rather than giving them assignments above or below their abilities.

You must also look for talents and abilities people do not use on the job, to open up possibilities for them to perform more effectively. Allowing an individual to work with his abilities gives him a feeling of adequacy and job identification. The greatest disservice to an employee is to underutilize his abilities.

We are not suggesting that you allow employees to experiment with their abilities, unguided and undirected. On the contrary, you must actively direct their talents and insights to help them expand their contributions to the needs of your organization.

Matching the Employee to the Job

One of industry's fundamental and often violated principles in the proper placement and utilization of people is matching the individual to the job. We all want the best person we can get, the ideal candidate. Typically, we hire a Ph.D. when a B.A. will do or a college graduate when a high school graduate will do. Unfortunately for both the man and the company, he will be unhappy at being underutilized. In such a mentally reductive situation an employee will either perform like a robot until he can find another job, or he may become a malcontent. Another reaction might be alcoholism or emotional illness resulting from task boredom.

Here the key question is, What does the job really require? When you have answered that, you can evaluate applicants on the basis of their skills and expectations.

SELF-IMAGE

Self-image is the picture we have inside ourselves that answers the question Who am I? It is the view we have of our self-worth and our role in life. Part of this self-image also is how we think others see us.

A key to effective leadership is the ability to relate to and operate with another person at the level of his self-image. Self-concept is the key factor in how people behave. People want to feel important to reinforce their self-esteem. If an assignment makes a man feel he is less a person than he likes to see himself, he will resist the task. But if the assignment reinforces his self-image, undergirding and building his view of himself, high motivation will be a natural outgrowth of effectively matching the assignment to the man and his self-worth.

Management used to feel that simply providing a man with a job entitled a company to gratitude and loyalty. Today, people are asking, "Is the assignment worthy of me?" A new and different generation is emerging, and it is important for managers to know what the new employees are seeking—and expecting. Their fathers wanted a job and a chance to bring home a dollar. Today's employees want more—a job that is worthy of them, an assignment that reinforces their self-esteem, building and supporting the notion of how they expect to be treated and used as individuals.

ETHICS AND MORALITY

One interesting aspect of organization behavior is how people can be encouraged or stifled, whether suggestions will be picked up or resisted—on the basis of people's concerns with ethics. People ask, "Is this ethical or moral? Does it fit *my* value system?"

In organization life people live closely together in a communal kind of existence. The community has a set of values, things held as having worth and meaning. These ethical considerations vary by class structure, economic group, industry, professional group, and so on. Group values, and the values held by individuals, form a backdrop against which all management decisions are judged.

The news media continually remind us of situations in which large corporations have violated either their own moral constraints or the constraints of the larger society in which they function. Stories abound of recalled automobiles, oil spills, price-fixing, kickbacks, and so on. Some organizations have gone out of existence or suffered serious financial losses because of violations of some of these ethical considerations and behavior constraints.

Right and Wrong

A moral management decision has many dimensions, and there is no textbook with a set of rules on how to behave. You must be a moral standard unto yourself. Ethical considerations are forced upon you as a trustee of the company's resources—money, men, and materials; it is a trust to be optimized, not wasted or destroyed.

Ethical standards are highly individualistic despite the fact that attitudes of what is right and wrong are culture-based. They are often also corporate-related. When you join a new company you should examine it as closely as you can to find out about the ethics of the people who work for that company. How does the company behave in its business practices? Can you live by its standards?

As a manager you should appreciate this highly individualistic perception of right and wrong. What tears one man up will not bother another. At this point we are not interested in demonstrating who is right or wrong in a particular situation. What has to concern us as members of management is the fact that certain things generate conflict in an individual's value system. Many times when a task request conflicts with a man's values, he may have a hard time telling you about it. It is your responsibility to get to know your employee's value systems.

Compromise

Most of us are willing to compromise on certain issues; some are willing to capitulate on almost any issue. However there is a point for nearly all of us beyond which we will not compromise, lie, or cover up. We all need to know that cutoff point.

We heard of a situation in which a director of a medical products company had to decide whether to take a product off the market. There were mixed reports of adverse reactions and only he had the power to decide. There were many pressures on this man: the product represented substantial sales and profits; the disease had no other adequate treatment; yet there was the possibility that the drug had severe negative consequences. The director pored over the research, agonized over it, and finally made the decision to withdraw the drug.

Not many of us have yet been put to the test. But when that time comes, you will find the point beyond which you cannot be pushed, and you will also learn the ethical lines of demarcation in those with whom you work.

Often in industry ethical questions are verbalized as either fitting or not fitting an individual's conscience. For example, suppose an engineer were asked to design a bridge. He knows that the structure will not handle the stress it is expected to, nor will it last the 70 or 90 years that it should. Yet his company demands that he underdesign this bridge to save money and time. If you were the engineer, would you compromise?

Responsibility

In this same example of the engineer, how many of us would rationalize our decision to build the bridge by saying "This is what the company wants; it is not my responsibility." If you would, then you have lost sight of your responsibility to yourself and to your management. If you are given an order to do something you feel is unethical, avoid the tendency to pass the buck, to be merely a soldier carrying out orders. You have to take a stand.

You cannot ask your subordinates to abdicate their moral responsibilities. If your people are not responding, it may be because you have inadvertently stepped on their silent values. Many people cannot talk about the convictions that are most central to their personality structure. You must make a conscious effort to become aware of their sensitivities and the pressures that are exerted by your authority.

MOTIVATION

Management must be concerned with optimizing return on investment (ROI). However, the concept of return on assets managed (ROAM) may more adequately describe the need to affect the growth of the enterprise. One of the largest assets, as well as the largest cost factor, in your management accountability is people. Through people you will either succeed or fail. The motivational variable, the directed energy commitment for turning ideas into action, is a critical part of the managing formula. Talent without motivation is the epitome of human waste. A person can have abilities, knowledge, and skills, and he can have everything going for him in the work environment, but if he is not motivated within himself to produce, the zest behind his behavior—and thus the achievement itself—will be minimal.

Motivation varies in content, degree of commitment, and direction. There are people who are motivationally set to respond in a certain direction, while others in the same situation will not respond in the same way. Motivation is tied to our attitudes, past experiences, self-images, and value judgments. We will be willing to commit our efforts in certain circumstances; our time, energy, and psychological gusto will be committed only when certain job assignments touch a motivational nerve, an area of value to us. Within each of us is a behavioral "pump." But that pump is primed, if you will, to do and not do certain things. The direction, as well as the intensity and our willingness to commit ourselves to do something, constitutes our motivation.

One of the basic features of motivation is that it resides within a person, not outside. It is not something that a manager does to people, or for people, or against people—coercion, manipulation, exploitation, herdsmanship, carrots and sticks. If you, as a manager, want people to move you can accomplish this quite easily. Movement is a response to the signals you give to indicate your desire in certain areas. But it should be remembered that conformance and performance are two different things. If you want "conformance movement," you need only to be physically bigger than the other person and to exercise the formal authority that comes with your title. But eventually people will rebel. They will leave you or they will do exactly what you want them to do but no more. If you want "performance movement," you must truly motivate a man by releasing what he already has inside himself, a self-generating power that all men have to some degree.

When asked how he had been able to sculpt the great beauty and power of David into a large slab of marble, Michelangelo replied that all he had done was *release* David from the rock. The David was already there, and it was only a matter of getting the chips out of the way. You must ask yourself what you can do to get the chips and stones out of the way so that your employees can give of themselves.

Anticipation Versus Reality

Motivation is greatly determined by how a new employee's job expectations correspond to the realities he finds in that job. His level of anticipation (LOA) is the total pattern of the expectations he has of the job situation. The level of reality (LOR) represents those things that actually exist in the job. We all have certain expectations when we first start a job. If we find that the realities are short of the expectations, there is a psychological space (or disappointment gap) between the LOA and the LOR. The difference between the two produces disharmony, disappointment, and dissonance. The greater the psychological space, the greater will be the frustration, disillusionment, irritation, and withholding of motivation. Conversely, the closer the realities of the job are to a man's anticipations and expectations, the greater will be his job satisfaction and the more motivation will be released through task identification.

Meaningful Work: A Prime Motivator

Motivation increases in relation to people's involvement with their work, and involvement increases with the meaningfulness of the work. If the work is worthwhile, has value, and gives an employee the opportunity to make a significant contribution to the company, and if the work contributes to his own self-interest, motivation will be high. But besides the meaningfulness of the work to the company, it is most important that it should contribute to his own self-interest. People need opportunities for real achievement, to give of themselves, to apply their skills and talents. Also, a job environment where a certain degree of failure is tolerated eliminates much of an employee's anxiety and enhances his motivation.

Motivation is also tied to a person's perception of the probable payoff in the form of recognition. If you do not provide people—particularly those with a high need for recognition—with acclaim and reinforcement when they have done a good job, you may seriously impair their motivation. When was the last time you received a memo saying that you had done a job well, with a copy sent to your boss? When was the last time you wrote such a memo to someone on your staff?

The manager who gives praise when praise is due is a motivation-releasing manager. The manager who provides recognition and reward in areas in which employees feel unsure or anxious is one who will reap the greatest rewards himself.

Encourage employees to share their ideas with you. If you really don't want their opinions, don't be phony. If you want to be autocratic, then go ahead and make unilateral decisions. But if you are genuinely concerned about people's feelings, interests, and ideas, let them know you want their suggestions.

As we have said, since motivation must come from within the individual, a manager cannot motivate anyone. He can only order and coerce people to do things. Such pressure works as long as you are there constantly to push, control, and nudge. But as soon as your back is turned, the will to work wanes. When people are self-motivated they produce without supervision. The willingness to work is something they give, not something you can demand of them.

The Need to Know

Just as people need to know why they are performing certain tasks and where such tasks will lead, they also need to know where they stand in your eyes. People need to know how procedural and personnel changes will affect them personally. They need personalized explanations about requests made of them so that they can focus on those aspects of their jobs that have the greatest self-reward factors. How you answer these needs determines how people will evaluate your leadership ability and the assignments that come from you. Most important to the motivational climate you create is an overriding sense of honesty. Your sincerity should be reflected in the individualized way you communicate with employees.

What all this boils down to is respect for human dignity and individual sensitivities. An individual should be treated in terms of his own problems and work needs in a climate of personalized attention and consideration. Everyone is preoccupied with his job life. If a manager bases his employee relations on respect for human dignity, he will be motivationally effective.

The Need to Grow

People need opportunity to grow and progress in fair competition with others. Not only are people self-extending but they will also strive to be better and more important than they are, to be a somebody rather than a nobody. Sometimes, out of our own need for control, power, or self-actualization, we forget that. If you are in management to dominate others, you will stifle your subordinates' motivation. Motivation stems from letting people grow and be independent, not from keeping them dependent.

SITUATION OPPORTUNITY

In any discussion of employee behavior it is important to examine the sociological as well as the psychological components of behavior. Our behavior is influenced by the social climate or work context. The work setting has both formal, clear-cut behavior norms as well as informal, even subjective standards. On the job we are exposed to group pressures that direct us to conform. The subtleties of group pressures on employees provide one of the most exciting areas for leadership effectiveness.

Within organized groups, particularly in corporate life, are many informal expectations that define behavior. Any infringement results in guilt or shame and often punishment by other members of the group. Some of the behavior you seek in your employees may violate group norms. For this reason, many in the group will resist certain assignments. They are not reluctant to perform because they don't want to or can't; they will not do the task because of the possible social consequences.

If you can get the employee group value system turned around by influencing the informal leader, the probability of your molding the group's attitudes and getting them to move in a certain direction will be increased.

Perception of Barriers

Some people always see problems as hurdles to be cleared, barriers to success, while others may perceive these very same circumstances as opportunities. Often neither barriers nor opportunities actually exist in the situation; it is a matter of how an individual perceives it.

The manager must be sensitive to these perceptions, give work in terms of them, and give employees the emotional support they need to get the job done. One of the greatest leadership challenges is determining whether to cast an assignment in such a way that the situation seems less threatening, or to help employees recast their perceptions. This preparation of the situation and the assignment must be done before you can expect the individual or the group in which he functions to be motivated in the desired direction. What is important is how the employee perceives the task.

RISK ORIENTATION

There are very few laws of behavior, particularly in the little-explored area of risk taking within organizations. Risk-taking behavior and the individual's orientation toward risk provide an interesting area for further personnel, psychological, and organization-process research. It is important because it helps determine whether people will behave as we hope they will or whether people will resist, become restless, and rebel against the manager's requests. The following discussion suggests hypotheses for research.

The accompanying matrix is a simple way to illustrate the hypothetical risk orientation of an individual in a specific situation. The left-hand label of the matrix indicates a factor or dimension of the situation (for example, perceived degree of success that can be attained). It should be noted that this is the person's own perception of the factor; it may not correspond to objective reality.

Willingness to Take Risk

	Low	High
Low	1	2
High	3	4

Factor/Dimension *

* The factor may be perceived probability of success, perceived task difficulty, perceived negative consequences, personal relevance, expected reward, or any other relevant aspect of the situation.

The person's perception of the factor or dimension, combined with his own willingness to take risks, may influence his behavior when he is offered a given task. This point can be best illustrated by inserting specific variables into the factor/dimension axis.

Success Versus Failure

Each of us has a certain degree of anxiety about the success or failure of any decision. Some employees are high risk takers; some employees are no-risk takers.

In this case, with the variable being the perception of success, we find some people who would be high risk takers even when there is a low probability of success (quadrant 2 in the matrix). They would be willing to expose themselves to failure even when there is little possibility of payoff. Others, on the other hand, might be willing to risk little even when there is a high probability of success in the venture (quadrant 3). People like that wear both suspenders and a belt in handling life choices.

Some people believe that success and failure are at opposite ends of the scale. Could it be that these really operate as two different dimensions—that some employees are *success seekers* and others are *failure avoiders*? Logic would dictate that when there is a high perception of probability of failure the smart thing for most of us is to proceed as low risk takers. Yet, very interestingly, some people are high risk takers even when there is a high probability of failure.

Task Difficulty

The perception of task difficulty is an important variable. One unusual thing about it is that task difficulty is assessed not only by its *inherent* difficulty, but also by a particular person's *perception* of the difficulty. A task is seen as easy or difficult on the basis of an individual's ability to perform it and on his emotional perceptions. High risk takers may accept a difficult task; low risk takers, even when their perception of task difficulty is low, won't chance failure.

Negative Consequences or Punishment

The relationship between the risk and the probability of negative consequences or punishment is another variable. Although some employees will take risks even when there is a high probability of being punished, willingness to take a risk may correlate with low probability of punishment.

Another related facet is the severity of the punishment and the probability of being punished. With people who are high risk takers, when there is a high probability of being punished, we would have to examine their perception of the severity of the punishment.

Personal Relevance and Reward

Some people take high risks because the task has personal significance. As people evaluate assignments, requests, and relationships, they are saying to themselves, "What's in it for me? What's in it for the people I care about? Is this assignment worth it to me?" Some people won't attempt an assignment that has no relevance at all to their self-interests.

Some people take high risks when there is a low probability of reward or when that reward is of low intensity or value. Conversely, some are low risk takers even when they see a high probability of reward in the assignment.

For managers, all these perceived risks represent important dimensions to be considered. Take them into account not only for yourself but also for your subordinates, particularly when you consider introducing changes. We perceive change as involving some level of risk. It may be a positive risk situation with positive consequences and gains, or it may have negative consequences.

Change also represents a degree of relevance or lack of relevance. To any new assignment we carry our previous orientations toward risk, either tending toward high risk taking or toward low risk or some gradient in between. The effective manager tries to mesh the assignment to each individual's own risk orientation and value system. To the extent this is possible, the probability increases that the assignment will be attempted.

Risk orientation probably changes as life situations change. Risk orientation may depend on age and life experience, on our health, our obligations, and our socioeconomic class. But it also depends on the special subjective ways we each perceive danger.

PERCEPTION OF AUTHORITY

Many managers spend their lives running from one job to another, only to find that they take their problems along. Part of this self-discovery is that there is always a boss—as the saying goes, no matter who you are, you are somebody else's peon. While that might seem too cynical, it is true that you have to cope effectively with authority in organizational living.

There seem to be three kinds of reactions to authority. One reaction is to *buck it*. Another is to *avoid it* by maintaining a distance. (Some employees send memos to the boss, hoping he will answer in writing.) The third reaction is to *circumvent* authority. This may stem from feeling uncomfortable or hostile with authority. That is why some people go over the boss's head or to other managers to form coalitions that will let them bring in heavy artillery to shoot from the side.

The effective, mature reaction to authority is to work within the boss's value system as well as your own. In organizations people must work things out together. People who move ahead generally have effective dialogues with those who have authority over them. They see that people in authority usually play a positive role and do not necessarily represent barriers.

Responsibility to People

People in positions of authority need to examine their interpersonal attitudes, especially immature managers who feel that authority in itself insures command. It is important to understand that real authority operates *with* others, not *over* others. As a manager you will be trying to get people to behave in a desired way, to get them to stop doing something, or to modify their actions in some way. Ask yourself if your use of authority facilitates that responsibility. Or does your use of authority merely remind people that they are subordinate to you?

Your employees needn't be reminded of who you are, but they do want to know what you expect of them, what you feel, and what your values are. To be effective in your administrative role, you must merit their cooperation, not demand it. If you order people to do things, you are saying that there is no other way for them to behave. In this display of power you probably are generating *conformance* rather than *performance*. Leadership is not exercising muscle or strong-arming people. Rather it should be an invitation to the other person to be the best he can. True influence and authority are gained through interpersonal exchange, not through acting out an egotistical need to flaunt power.

Your Boss's Authority

As you further your own career, your perception of authority will be extremely important. In any job it is important to have a strong boss because you need his power and support so that together you can make things happen. If you work for a weak man both he and you will suffer in the informal organization.

MANAGEMENT BY OBJECTIVES

Management by objectives is a management philosophy that has great influence on communication and motivation. To induce change in a desired, predictable way, a manager should provide his subordinate with an opportunity to enter the arena as a co-opting manager. We share our task-defining role and we must understand his values and work needs. Further, we mutually interact with our employees so that *together* we set goals for work output and activity. With this philosophy we establish objectives, not simply programs.

As a manager you must accomplish certain things for your department, division, and company in relation to its markets. But you also want certain things for yourself; you have a set of expectations you would like to fulfill through your job. Hopefully, you will be able to find pleasure in your work, job excitement, and a feeling of identification in doing the work required to accomplish your objectives and those of the company.

Leadership should be a mutual sharing, planning, and goal-setting process, not a routine personnel procedure. Management by objectives allows for this interaction. Before we can expect behavior change, or influence over employee behavior, we need to communicate our expectations. We must invest time, time to learn the perceptions, work values, and objectives of our employees. Then we must identify the objectives, needs, and values of our corporation. As managers, we must blend these expectations to optimize the payoff to the company as well as to the individual. This is accomplished by *mutually defining* the goals, objectives, values, and expectations that you have for the other person. We do not surrender the objectives of the company to the whims of the employee. We make a deliberate inventory of the employee's thinking so that we can better mesh his objectives with those of the company. This matching and blending process produces results for all concerned.

All of us function in a subordinate role. Each of us has a boss, and each of us wants to win his praise. In the subordinate role one continuing concern is trying to determine what it takes to please the old man, what it takes to relieve the anxieties that you have about his expectations of you. The answer to that comes through confrontation, sincerity, and management by objectives.

People can't begin to behave effectively until they know clearly what is wanted in a particular situation. Management often complains of poorly motivated employees, when the fact is the employees are willing to perform if only someone would tell them what is desired and what is expected of them. They must also be told what not to do, especially in critical areas. We should always be consciously aware that people not only want to survive on the job; they also want meaningful jobs. They are willing to give it all they have if someone at the managerial level will tell them just what is wanted. Management by objectives is based on clarity of communication, and it takes time to affirm and reinforce that communication link.

The prevailing value system must also be communicated. The other individual must climb inside your value system to see how it fits his. He has to know what has value for you. It is your values, perceptions, and attitudes that to a large extent will determine his behavior.

If all the factors in the behavioral formula check out—if an employee is motivationally geared up, if he works well with authority, if he is willing to take risk, if his past experience is positive and contributory, and if the ethical values are aligned with yours—but he doesn't understand what you want, then his performance will suffer and he will be frustrated.

Many human variables influence behavior. These variables interact and assume different psychological weight, depending on the individual person and the particular situation in which he operates. On the surface many variables appear unrelated and free-floating. For the astute manager—the manager who systematically understands his people through these dimensions—there should emerge increasing predictability that will allow him to better forecast the direction in which his employees will go. Through sensitivity to the variables that affect human behavior, the manager will not only solve his people problems; he will also fully achieve his organization's objectives, his own career goals, and the needs of his employees.

3

Organization Effectiveness

Samuel Beckett wrote that often "life ends long before death." This statement could be applied to many companies today. Maybe the concern you are working for has long lost its vitality and only awaits final interment. Often the sad story can be explained by one simple word: ineffectiveness—organization ineffectiveness.

What is organization effectiveness? It is the extent to which an organization, with defined and finite resources, can achieve its growth and profit without destroying its internal resources. It is how a company meets its objectives with its available assets. Organization effectiveness is the minimization of slippage between the input of resources and the optimized output.

Perhaps we can understand by analogy, by recalling Ralph Sockman's statement concerning a ship:

There are parts of a ship which taken by themselves would sink. The engine would plunge to the bottom of the sea and so would the propeller. The steel of the hull would sink. But when the parts of the ship are put together they float.

Organization effectiveness is "getting it all together" to keep the enterprise afloat and competitive. This chapter discusses some of those factors involved in effectiveness.

EMPLOYEES

An organization's effectiveness focuses not only on finances and work productivity, but also on the employee system that makes it go. *The competitive edge that any company has is its human resources.* Capital equipment and physical facilities can be purchased by the competitor down the street. A first consideration, then, is the effectiveness, as well as the subsequent efficiency, of the personnel that cause the organization ship to sink or to float. The real swing factor is the effectiveness of the managers and directors who lead and release the motivation of their employees within the organization's social system. Are the quarterbacks and other players any good?

GOALS

The health and growth of the organization are based on the clear identification, commitment to, and communication of goals, and how each subcomponent of the company contributes to those goals. Often organization objectives are not interrelated; frequently they conflict. The organization without interlocked goals and objectives can be compared to a ship—this time without a rudder—adrift on the marketplace ocean, blown hither and yon by reactive winds and tides. A floundering corporation becomes reactive rather than proactive and is at the mercy of situational events. We see company environments that are receptive yet devoid of guidance and self-determination. The opposite also exists, that is, closed, rigid organization systems insensitive to growth opportunities and incapable of reacting to them. Such organizations tend to make a virtue of the status quo, living on past glory—and diminishing profit from existing product lines. Emphasis is on paternalistic maintenance of present personnel rather than the active development of new managerial talent to keep the organization competitive and alive to its future growth.

ADAPTABILITY

Another measure of an organization's effectiveness is its ability to adapt to changing opportunities by developing sensors to pick up and relay changes in the system, whether those changes be threats or opportunities.

Parallel to this is the adaptation of personnel within the organization: the recruitment of new talent, the removal of unsatisfactory and marginal performers, and the reassignment of talented personnel so as to optimize their contributions in another part of the system for their own welfare as well as for that of the organization. It is both a personal and a corporate loss when highly talented individuals cannot obtain reassignment to jobs that make better use of their abilities. These people leave the company for job-enriched alternatives outside. It is not uncommon for one subsystem of an organization to be in dire need of new talent while another subsystem is losing the very employee who could fill the bill.

Within any group structure, be it a family setting or a conglomerate corporation, a certain amount of dissent and conflict exist. Effectiveness depends on a healthy attitude in confronting the conflict. The organization that balks and denies internal conflict is remiss, because it loses an opportunity for constructive change.

COMMUNICATION

In spite of the formal as well as the informal setup for open and direct communication of change, valuable suggestions for change are often lost. An overcontrolling environment and bureaucratic rituals tend to choke off and destroy inputs from employees and stifle the flow of ideas. While organization effectiveness pivots around managerial control to assure that work productivity is directed toward the accomplishment of objectives, overcontrol has as its price the loss of initiative and creativity.

The manager's systems, projects, and departmental control must not clog the organization's arteries for change. But the opposite conditions are just as damaging. An organization without effective controls has no way of evaluating deviations from standards of performance. Managers need to manage, to listen, and to control within the framework of open and trustful relationships so that employees can effectively influence their working situation and provide new alternatives. Managing is a process of mutual influence, exercised by people at all levels within the organization.

Job Descriptions

An important dimension of organization effectiveness is the clarity of job descriptions and the resultant authority to make commitment. Job descriptions based on reality are essential to effective work. They draw attention to the need for updating a man's job accountabilities and output expectations on a 12- to 18-month basis against agreed-upon standards of performance.

A good job description makes explicit what authority the employee has to commit resources and the point beyond which he will need approval to make a decision. In organizations where there is lack of position clarity, there is upward delegation. The emphasis is on control, with a serious lack of clarity about authority and responsibility. Delegated and fixed assignments without authority and power to implement action are useless and a sign of a non-action-oriented organization.

To be effective, people need legitimization, specific communication, and mutual agreement concerning their power to make a commitment to the objectives for which they are responsible. In those organizations where power, influence, and authority are not legitimized at lower levels, management will have difficulty evaluating just who is a performer and who is not. Furthermore, there is uncertainty about action and implementation that generates a climate of excuse making and marginal initiation of action. Lack of employee initiative may well be a by-product of a punishing environment in which there is no specificity about one's authority to act.

MANPOWER DEVELOPMENT

An organization's effectiveness and future hinge on a systematic manpower planning and development process. An organization must attend to the motivational aspects of employees' identification with their present jobs, and it must also devise a systematic process to identify those people who are vertically career oriented and who have the capability for increased managerial accountabilities. Systematic manager development is the organization lifeline. Systematic manager-succession planning for both organization and individual management development can meet growth needs as well as the contingency losses that occur through death, disability, termination, and early retirement.

Organization development and systematic management development processes are no longer a luxury service for companies that expect to be viable and competitive for years to come. It is vital to an organization's continuity to insure that the decision makers of tomorrow will have the potential to meet the evolving challenges. To assume leadership and meet the long-range growth plan of an organization require talented, readied, backup personnel. Those with managerial potential should be identified early so their systematic grooming can begin. The recruitment of new managerial blood into the system, with alternative viewpoints about organization opportunities, is also important. Manpower planning fails when it does not address itself to the early, systematic recruitment and internal development of managerial candidates.

ORGANIZATION SELF-CONCEPT

Another earmark of an effective organization is its self-concept. Many organizations survive only by managing crisis after crisis, by being reactive, barely giving a thought to its own internal values and reasons for being. Every organization needs to look at itself and at its values. Its objectives, standards of performance, and goals are predicated on knowing its self-concept. Often considerable funds are allocated to a multitude of issues external to the organization rather than to internal public relations. The result is that employees and managers not conversant with company values frequently flounder in trying to second-guess what decision-making posture should be taken.

In the effective organization, values are known and communicated with regularity. An organization with no self-concept is open to confusion; its managers become suspect and uncomfortable with no clear values for their operating decisions. Psychologically they may become hesitant and withdraw from the decision-making process. Psychological punishment may result from a lack of compliance to organization self-concepts and values. Employees and managers in such a free-floating system are reluctant to make a commitment for action when they do not know what will be rewarded and what will be penalized. In this type of politico-reactive environment, cohesion is threatened; individuals go their own way in their search for the relevant. Employees are filled with anxiety since they cannot determine which values are reinforced and which are not.

INFORMATION SHARING

An effective organization is characterized by communication networks where information exchange can be rapid, reliable, and reciprocal. Operating managers need open and trustful information exchange. Where there is complexity or confusion in information networks, managers tend to restrict information for political and organizational protection. In a degenerating organization, information exchange is minimal, suspect, and guarded. One method of evaluating an organization is to ask each employee whether he has adequate information to handle his job and what kind of information he requires to be more effective.

A successful organization is noted by the healthy ability to confront threat and opportunity, both internally and externally. If that is lacking, it may be because of misunderstanding due to broken links of communication that act as barriers to the free flow of information needed by another unit. This criterion is particularly important for geographically decentralized organizations. The achievement potential of the organization, as well as its integration, are dependent upon the open and rapid exchange of information needed by work stations where immediate action is required. Only through open communication links can the defined ideology of a company be congruent with its priorities for production.

ORGANIZATION EVOLUTION

The first stage of a corporation's life is usually characterized by great enthusiasm and the ability to take risks in struggling for a share of its market. During the second stage it may have to deal with internal conflicts and differences of opinion about its self-concept. In the third stage it must take a hard look at internal effectiveness and marketplace profitability. This should result in a reshaping of the system for entry onto a higher learning curve. The last stage of organization evolvement also focuses on increased market penetration with more sophisticated marketing techniques and better identification and use of people. There will also be a clearer definition of goals and the legitimization of authority. Its managers will have become toughened and professional.

An organization dies if it fails to adapt to a changing environment, to cope with conflict, or to respond rapidly to marketplace demands. A successful organization must constantly offer a wide range of responses to the various stimuli in the environment. This sort of company, supported by adaptable, capable managers armed with a repertoire of ways in which to meet both opportunity and threat, must place high value on performance effectiveness rather than efficiency per se. While efficiency in the internal routines may follow from organization effectiveness, seldom does effectiveness follow internal efficiency. A viable organization accepts challenge, is positive toward change, and allocates its resources flexibly in a changing situation.

In all stages of corporate life, managerial personnel must be alerted to marketplace opportunities to prevent any tendency toward inward myopic perceptions. A factor that distinguishes a living organization from a deteriorating one is its willingness to reassess its own policies when they have become rigid and stifling. Having defined position tasks is one thing; the arteriosclerosis which occurs when an organization is bogged down and overly structured is quite another. An organization should be flexible and free to commit itself to new directions.

PERFORMANCE FEEDBACK

The immediacy and accuracy of performance feedback provide nutrients and healthy soil to generate and perpetuate organization growth and performance. Just as organizations need to constantly calculate their position relative to their goals, employees want to know where they stand. Both the organization and the individual require vehicles for accurate and relevant performance feedback. Toward those ends, an organization should devote time and care to monitoring its performance feedback loops. Otherwise everyone operates in a void—an organizational fog.

As an organization approaches its final stage of evolution, there is a tendency to overstaff. The effective organization will prevent proliferation of unneeded staff experts. Instead, at this stage, the company must centralize operations for greater accessibility to the autonomous units. The return on investment from staff experts must be monitored through charge-back billing for services rendered. Staff personnel must pay for their existence, their salary, and other generated costs.

For example, the effective organization is concerned with the ratio of line management (direct-cost personnel) to the indirect charges borne by line managers for internal experts. Centralization of staff makes the cost, as well as the contribution, of these professionals visible. Staff personnel should know that they will be held accountable for their contribution to the corporate goals. They should account to line management for services rendered, services that are based on standards of performance and that provide a means for evaluating their real contribution.

Often an outside consultant can provide greater ROI in a more immediate and demonstrative way, obviating the frequent need for the services of an inside group of experts. Each organization must regularly evaluate the increase of its staff to determine whether, compared with the cost generated, there is a greater ROI from its services.

PLANNING

Effective organization planning tends to be on a relatively long time scale. The annual gadflying of long-range planning is superior to casual, day-to-day reactiveness.

There is much discussion in the management literature about the advantages of bottom-to-top planning as opposed to unilateral planning from the top. Planning and strategic decision making can be made in both ways within the organization setting. In an ineffective organization there is often a watering down and a catch-as-catch-can approach as to which managers are responsible for planning. As an organization evolves, long-range planning should increasingly involve those individuals on lower levels who can make a meaningful contribution to those plans. Tactical decision making should be delegated as far down as practical in the organization, thus providing a launch pad for the implementation of objectives.

In an ineffective organization planning is too dispersed; too many people who have little or no relevant contribution to make are invited to contribute. Often such people are invited only for status reasons.

AN ACHIEVING CLIMATE

Organization effectiveness is determined by managerial and executive climate. Many arthritic and stagnant organizations have lost a kind of élan or atmosphere of achievement. When people are not expected to perform with excellence and are deprived of meaningful performance feedback, the environment regresses to mediocrity. A result-producing climate will be marred when employees are encumbered by executive pessimism or burdened with routine tasks that should be automated or eliminated from the system. In status quo organizations employees are maintained simply to be busy.

The effective organization generates an achieving climate wherein both managers and employees have a sense of urgency, responsibility, and real freedom to execute those responsibilities. The effective organization expects achievement, and rewards results, not efforts.

When a manager expects excellence there is an increased probability that he will get it. Conversely, when managers set minimum standards they elicit a regression to mediocre standards of performance.

An achieving organization climate is characterized by clarity of objectives and a freedom to capitalize upon competitiveness and the drive for mastery. Rather than harnessing employees, this climate releases them; it encourages and facilitates their optimum performance.

When jobs are enriched by meaningfulness, and are surrounded by a climate that expects excellence, an organization's vitality increases. One of management's prime responsibilities is to focus attention on the confrontation of current realities, not preoccupation with what should have been or might have been. Organizations become neurotic and paranoid just as people do; they develop a basic defensiveness—a wall of protection—that inhibits any spirit of achievement. As you evaluate your organization, ask yourself whether the climate is ad hoc and participatory or whether the managers wring their hands over the past.

Organization élan, the spirit of achievement, is based on the integration of organization and employee goals—that is, a congruence between the organization's objectives and individual interests and talents. Such a congruence engenders a closer identification of the employee with the system. A climate of achievement is also generated by mutual trust and goal setting between the employee and his immediate manager.

MANAGERIAL ECOLOGY

"Managerial ecology"—that is, management's concern with ethical excellence—is a cornerstone of organization effectiveness. The modern, effective organization must concern itself with the impact of its actions on the social and physical world around it. Ethics weigh heavily on today's corporate conscience. Companies feel that they must stand *for* something, not just be *against* something. Each organization must take the time to define its reason for being, its self-concept, and the ways in which it will and will not do business (both with its employees and with the general public). Day-in, day-out decision making should emanate directly from the values and priorities a company sets for its own behavior.

Getting it all together to make the corporate ship a buoyant entity—that's what organization effectiveness is about.

4

Before the Union Knocks

One indicator of a company's viability in dealing with the dynamics of its human organization is its approach to its plant and office employees. The ineffective organization fails to respond to legitimate grievances, demotivates and demoralizes its human assets by inequitable treatment, and adopts repressive tactics against employees. Some managements adopt a nihilistic philosophy that unionism is inevitable, if they are presently nonunion, or that it will spread to white collar workers if plant employees are already unionized. Effective management can prevent unionization by aggressively adopting tactics which will result in organization renewal and the proper utilization of human resources.

Historically, the union movement has been one of organized rebellion against management and its practices by employees who felt that a change in the balance of power was needed. Unionization is primarily a defensive move on the part of the worker group to protect itself from management abuses. In the present era of lush fringe benefit programs and high wage levels, the motivation for the genesis of the labor movement is too often forgotten. It is very easy and simplistic to label unionists

This chapter is adapted with permission from "Unionism and the Non-Union Company," *Personnel Journal*, June 1969.

as agitators, power grabbers, and whited sepulchers. But the fact remains that the same precipitating causes that generated labor revolts nearly a century ago are still to be found in many nonunion situations today.

Basically, unionization is caused by management failure. This failure is usually composed of many elements: some economic, some having to do with interpersonal relationships, and some with meaningfulness of work. But in every case of unionization, management has either failed to understand employee needs and wants, or has failed to act in a way which would fulfill these wants.

Is such conflict inevitable? Karl Marx saw the conflict which existed between workers and management in the sweatshops of England, and concluded that the only way for workers to satisfactorily resolve the problem was to forcibly seize the means of production by political revolution. The problem remains one of staggering dimensions. But modern-day knowledge of the psychological and sociological factors operative in such a situation can permit a more peaceful means of resolving worker dissatisfactions.

It should be obvious that the best way for management to prevent unionization is to offer employees those things offered to them by the union. Yet this best strategy is often overlooked by managers who seek to keep the union out by legal strategems while maintaining the status quo as far as its labor practices are concerned. Such shortsighted tactics do nothing more than forestall the inevitable.

In light of what we have come to know about people and their need for growth opportunities and development, it is obvious that the work people do is of great significance. In work is to be found the key to motivation and worker satisfaction. There is a growing failure in the industrial world which threatens today's manager: It is the failure of employees to find satisfaction in the work they do. Why is there such a high rate of turnover and unhappiness on the job? And why, in the case of unionized employees, is there such open hostility against management? What is the root cause of the conflict between the employee's expectations and values and those held by the company?

Prior to the Industrial Revolution, and for a long time following it, there was for the vast majority a close and intimate relationship between a man and his work. Very often the man grew his own raw materials, fashioned them into some type of usable item, and marketed the final product. The entire process was in his hands. Associated with the act of creation was the man's sense of pride, and in this sense men spoke of themselves as craftsmen. There was a purpose, a sense of unity, a feeling of accomplishment about work.

But in our modern industrial world man is separated from the meaning of his work, or more correctly, he sees no meaning in his work. This alienation has ramifications in several areas:

1. *Powerlessness.* A person is powerless when he is an object controlled and manipulated by other persons or by an impersonal system (such as technology) and when he cannot assert himself as a subject to change or modify this domination.

2. *Meaninglessness.* Work is seen as meaningless when a person's individual acts seem to have no relation to a broader life program (the cog-in-the-machine effect). Meaninglessness also occurs when individual roles are not seen as fitting into the total system of goals of the organization.

3. *Isolation.* A third characteristic of alienation from work is a fragmentation of the individual away from society. "Isolation" suggests the idea of general societal alienation—the feeling of being in, but not of, society, of being remote from collective efforts. The trend toward isolation is illustrated by rising divorce rates and family disintegration.

4. *Self-estrangement.* When work becomes a means to an end, rather than an end in itself, man becomes separated from that which gives meaning to much of life. When work is self-estranging, when it is a means rather than a fulfilling end, one's occupation does not contribute in an affirmative manner to personal identity and selfhood, but instead is damaging to self-esteem.

Self-estrangement also involves a separation of work from other concerns. Hence, Henrik Ibsen in *A Doll's House* could write of the industrialist who compartmentalized his life, with family, work, church, mistress, and so on all separated from each other, and with no continuity of experience. This schizophrenic relationship has been introduced into the life of modern man primarily by the work environment, though it finds reinforcement in much of modern life.

These fragmentations in man's experience all seem to have resulted from basic changes in social organization brought about by the Industrial Revolution. That is why the alienation concept has a peculiarly modern ring. Few people in preindustrial societies seem to be alienated. But in a bureaucratic mass society, huge numbers of people show signs of alienation.

Thus the problem for management is one of overcoming the deadening effects of alienation, or at least rendering these effects bearable for individuals and relatively harmless for society. Despite the common features of modern employment situations, industrial environments vary markedly in their alienating tendencies. Whether a worker approaches the state of feeling he is a commodity, a resource, or a cost element in the production process depends on his relation to technology, the social structure of his industry, and its economic fortunes. The industry in which a man works is significant here, because the conditions of work and existence in various industrial environments are quite different. But the universal problem facing a manager who is interested in preventing unionization is how to change the work environment to satisfy personal needs without sacrificing production.

Why do employees join unions? For money? For fringe benefits? Herzberg, Myers, and others have shown that money serves as a base upon which worker satisfaction is built, but that money itself does not satisfy. If wages are not at acceptable levels, workers will be dissatisfied; but increasing wages will not buy worker satisfaction.

The theme which underlies in-depth analysis of a worker's reasons for joining a union is that work is not meaningful and the worker is not treated as an individual. Consider this quotation from a worker in relation to his job environment:

I feel like a vegetable. I do the same damn thing day in and day out. I want to transfer out of there. Every time I tell my supervisor about the way I feel he reminds me of the money I'm making. He just doesn't understand that what I really want is a job I enjoy doing.

Or this worker's alienation from his work:

When that 5 o'clock whistle blows, I run to my car. I can't wait to escape that place, and I dread coming in in the morning. Putting seven bolts in the rear quarter panel of a Chevy truck day after day just isn't inspiring work.

The worker's need to find meaning, importance, and creativity in his work is perhaps the hardest message to convey to management.

WHAT UNIONS PROMISE EMPLOYEES

Unions are powerless *if* management already supplies to its employees those items which unionists say they can offer. In election campaigns unions have traditionally employed a variety of appeals that serve as a good checklist. If company programs and policies are deficient in any of the following areas, management is extending an open invitation for trouble. The most common union appeals:

1. Seniority rights will be protected. The long-service employee is assured of preferential treatment.
2. Better communication between employees, and communication between employees and management, are promised. Employees are promised that they will be kept "in the know" and not in the dark.

3. Employee morale will be improved; job frustration and lack of direction will be remedied.

4. More responsible attitudes on the part of management will be fostered. Management will be concerned about the employees' desires.

5. Employees will be more involved in the affairs of the business. They will participate in the running of day-to-day operations and in the decision-making process.

6. Greater personal development, self-actualization, and creativity on the job will be nurtured. People will not be held back, but allowed to grow and progress.

7. Better wages and more equitable salary administration will be assured.

8. Broader coverage of benefit programs is promised.

9. Uniform application of company policies and justice and orderly treatment for all employees are promised.

10. Performance of management will be improved. Employees disgusted with sloppy management are told the union will make management shape up.

11. Democracy will be introduced in the work place; authoritarian rule will be overturned.

12. Unions will promote policy changes, and will function as a change agent in a relatively stagnant situation.

13. Grievances against management will be processed. The employee will be granted a court of appeal instead of serving as a pawn. The union will act as his advocate.

14. Working conditions will be improved. The environment will be better and better tools and equipment will be provided.

15. Employee unity will be strengthened. The union is in a real sense a fraternity, a brotherhood.

16. Job security will be provided. Employees may not be fired at whim.

17. Promotion and transfer practices will be clear-cut.

It would appear that if management were alert to the above points, there would be no need for a union. Unfortunately, too many members of top management have assumed that their employees see the work environment from management's perspective, whereas they actually see it from an entirely different viewpoint. Management further assumes that if it hears no complaints, there are no complaints. Such assumptions are, of course, false and dangerous. Management must know where areas of difficulty are and move into them quickly.

As Professor Daniel Katz has pointed out, three basic strategies can be used to deal with conflicts between labor and management.

1. Make the system work. (Are current personnel policies effective?)
2. Develop additional machinery for conflict adjudication.
3. Restructure the organization to reduce built-in conflict.

No one approach will be sufficient. Perceptive managements will use an eclectic approach and take from each those elements that will best form an intelligent organizational solution.

MAKING THE SYSTEM WORK

Management, in its tripartite approach to the prevention of unionization, should first focus on ways to improve existing procedures, practices, and relationships. Too often, programs are established but allowed to lapse into complete ineffectiveness. Areas that seem to be most important include:

Communication

Ralph Nichols, chairman of the Department of Rhetoric at the University of Minnesota, and one of the outstanding consultants in the field of industrial communications, has produced evidence indicating that communication upward from employees to top management is virtually nonexistent. Downward communication from top management to the employee through five levels of management results in only 20 percent understanding by the employee group. What can be done to improve communication?

1. *Attitude surveys.* Top management does not know what the employee group thinks—and, more importantly, does not know what it feels. A survey of employees' opinions should be made periodically. As a side benefit, management often reaps the Hawthorne effect; employees are made to feel important simply by having their opinions sought.

2. *"Gripe" boxes.* An anonymous method of employee communication with management must be provided. Management must take action when there is legitimate cause for a gripe. If questions are asked, they must be answered fully and truthfully. A recent survey concerning the operation of one plant's gripe-box system revealed widespread worker dissatisfaction with supervision, company policies, and wage administration. The report concluded with the information that the only action management took was to install a water cooler. If an organization operates in this manner, the worker soon learns that management is not serious about wanting to communicate.

3. *Employee interviews.* Employees should be interviewed periodically by members of immediate supervision and by higher levels of management if possible. At IBM, every employee is interviewed each year by a member of management at least two levels above the employee's supervisor. Higher levels of management are thus kept in closer contact with the feelings of employees at lower levels.

4. *Media usage.* It is necessary that the employee feel in on things. Bulletin boards, the company newspaper, and employee handbooks are some ways to communicate what is happening within the company. Employee group meetings and weekly meetings with supervision are effective ways to communicate personally. Though time consuming, these are a necessary part of the communication picture.

Underlying any tactical move on the part of management to increase the flow of communication must be a realization of the obstacles to communication, some of which are:

1. Many employees fear that expressing their true feelings about the company to their boss could be dangerous.
2. There is a fairly widespread belief that disagreeing with the boss will block promotion.
3. There is a widespread conviction that because management is remote from employees, it is not interested in employee problems.
4. Many employees feel that they are not rewarded for good ideas.
5. Supervisors are often felt to be inaccessible and unresponsive.
6. Employees have the conviction that higher management doesn't take prompt action on problems.

Improvement of Supervision

To the individual employee the company is represented by his unit, and management by his supervisor. In case after case of nonunion plants going union, much of the responsibility can be laid at the door of poor supervision. For example, many of the barriers to communication mentioned above can be overcome only with the help of effective supervision. Rensis Likert referred to the supervisor as the "linkpin" who ties the individual employee into the organization and its purposes. If this linkpin is weak, the employee is isolated and cut off, and generally rebels. Improvement of supervision can be accomplished in a variety of ways:

1. *Selection.* It is not logical to assume that a good worker will make a good supervisor. If he has poor interpersonal relationships, management is taking a gamble in placing him in a position of authority.

2. *Supervisory training.* In-house training in supervisory skills such as interviewing and counseling should be provided, in addition to schooling in company procedures.

3. *Evaluation.* Surprisingly, many industries still have no form of supervisory evaluation. The supervisor who does not communicate, who does not listen, who does not develop his people or take an active interest in them, is a liability to any company.

Employee Evaluation and Salary Administration

Employee appraisal is one of the never-never lands in the world of industry. It almost never takes place, and when it does it is seldom effective. Too often, the employee is rated on the basis of personality traits which, for most jobs, have very little to do with the work he performs. There has also been little effort to tie the worker's performance to pay levels. Managers seem to be missing an obvious point here: Since the employee is supposed to get paid for what he does, there must be a linking between performance and pay. Bell Laboratories has pioneered in this area with a computer-programmed salary administration procedure that is directly related to employee rankings.

In analyzing employee performance, the following points seem to have relevance:

1. Evaluations should be held periodically, at least once a year, on a schedule known to the employee.

2. The employee should know what his supervisor's expectations are in advance of the evaluation interview, and on what items he will be rated (hopefully the employee has had some voice in establishing the rating procedure). "Surprises" are not good form.

3. The written performance review should be read by the employee and signed, and a copy given to the employee for his records. A discussion of the review should be held.

4. An employee who is dissatisfied with the evaluation should be able to appeal his rating through a grievance procedure.

5. The employee should be evaluated on a group basis, with the immediate supervisor's evaluation being reviewed by higher levels of management.

6. The evaluation is not under any circumstances to be used as a substitute for weekly meetings, which are used for communication and problem solving. It is a time to review the employee's performance and to set objectives that will help him to improve.

Job Promotion and Transfer

The worker dissatisfied with his present job, or desiring to better himself by promotion, usually finds that information about job openings is restricted. Lack of information and ignorance of opportunity breed distrust and suspicion. Employees need to know not only where they stand, but where they can go. Job posting is a union invention designed to provide interested employees with information concerning openings. Employees then bid for positions, with seniority being given prime consideration.

Posting can also be adopted in the nonunion plant. There is no legitimate reason why employees should be kept in the dark as to their chances for advancement. Features of a nonunion job-posting system might include:

1. All available jobs would be posted.
2. Employees would notify the personnel department of their interest. This is an important element. Many nonunion posting systems have the employee notify the supervisor of their interest, and he in turn is supposed to relay the employee's request to personnel. Many employees will be deterred from expressing interest if they have to approach supervision.
3. Supervision would be notified of an employee's interest only if he were interviewed for an opening.
4. Personnel would screen all applicants, and refer those who were qualified. Each employee who expressed interest would be notified of the disposition of his request.
5. As a supplement to employees' expressions of interest, supervisors would recommend candidates they feel to be qualified.

Management's policies are not the issue here (although there is always room for improvement); the issue is how those policies are implemented. Frequently, the causes of worker dissatisfaction stem from practices and procedures that do not effectively answer employees' needs for full information, concerned supervision, economic equity, and growth opportunity. In its campaign to win worker loyalty, management must begin by turning into reality that which it too often only talks about.

DEVELOPING ADDITIONAL MACHINERY FOR CONFLICT ADJUDICATION

The second part of management's three-pronged attempt to prevent unionization has to do with conflict resolution within the organization. One of the union organizer's most effective appeals is the promise that the union will bring into the work situation an effective grievance procedure. Such a procedure, with the weight of the union behind it, will offset the power of management and allow the employee to be heard.

The management myth still persists that the employee should feel free to consult his supervisor at any time about any problem. One might cynically say that the motherly policies of the corporation are supposed to team with the father-supervisor to mete out fair and impartial justice to the employee-child. But it just isn't so. In actual fact, the employee, because he lacks power in the work environment, does not take grievances to supervision, but bottles up his frustration or spreads discord among fellow employees. The executive ulcer has its correlate in the worker bad back and allergy problem.

How can a company establish a work atmosphere in which employees will not feel it necessary to be represented by a "third party" (to use a rather euphemistic management phrase)? In a nonunion plant, complaints and grievances are too often ignored or smothered. A formalized grievance procedure is a necessary part of the solution to this continuing problem. Professor Neal Drought of Temple University recommends a policy which "guarantees each employee the right to register a grievance and to process it through well-defined steps up to the top man, without fear of either direct or indirect reprisal."[1] Through such a policy the employee is able to raise his hand, call attention to himself, and at least present his case in hope of a solution favorable to himself.

Another important point is that anxieties caused by the work situation can find expression in the grievance procedure. Such a procedure, where the worker can "get it off his chest," must be capable of circumventing the employee's supervisor. It is important that there be a written grievance procedure which is publicized to all employees. Unfortunately, employees will not often use it. It is evident on a moment's contemplation, and experience confirms, that few (if any) employees will avail themselves of a management-established grievance procedure. The majority of employees are only too acutely aware of the many direct and indirect means available to their immediate supervisors to retaliate against subordinates who incur their displeasure, especially by initiating a grievance which may reflect on the fairness or competence of the supervisor.

Such retaliation, the employee fears, may take the form of withholding an otherwise deserved merit increase, being bypassed for promotion, having one's proportionate overtime hours reduced, being assigned the next six undesirable jobs that come along, being subjected to persistent

---

[1] "Grievances in the Non-union Situation," *Personnel Journal*, June 1967, p. 332. We are indebted to Professor Drought for much of the thinking in this area of discussion.

criticisms and harassment, or even being discharged on trumped-up charges.

But the very availability of such a grievance procedure has the psychological advantage of displaying management's intention to provide for the equitable resolution of grievances. This ancillary advantage makes it worthwhile.

A Proposed Grievance Procedure

A grievance procedure, in order to be effective, must contain the following elements (see also the accompanying diagram):

1. Three to five steps of appeal (depending upon the size of the organization). Three steps will usually be sufficient.
2. A written account of the grievance should be made if it goes past the first level in the appeal process. This facilitates communications and defines the issue at hand.
3. Alternate routes of appeal should be open to the employee so that the supervisor can be circumvented. (The personnel department is the most logical alternate route.)
4. A time limit on each step of the appeal should be established so that the employee has some expectation of when he can expect an answer.
5. The system must have the support of all levels of management so that it is not emasculated.
6. The employee must have the right to ask one or two fellow employees to accompany him. This safety-in-numbers approach helps to overcome his fear of reprisal.
7. If the employee demonstrates that he has a rightful grievance, it must be acted upon (there has to be "bite" in the system if it is to gain the respect of employees and members of supervision).
8. Both management and employee have the right to appeal to a higher level.

The union offers a final step in the grievance procedure that has been difficult for the nonunion plant to duplicate: arbitration. Scandinavian countries have contributed the intriguing notion of the ombudsman who has power to resolve conflicts between citizens and the state. The corporate ombudsman (sometimes an outsider) as an impartial neutral is a healthy move in the right direction. Not entangled in loyalties to either management or labor, but feeling responsible to both, he is able to act as a court of final judgment which keeps the solution to the problem within the family circle. The secret of success here is that dirty linen is not washed in public.

A GRIEVANCE SYSTEM FOR THE NONUNION COMPANY.

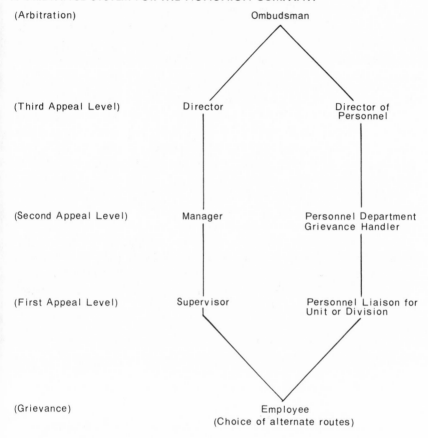

(Arbitration)   Ombudsman

(Third Appeal Level)   Director   Director of
                                                           Personnel

(Second Appeal Level)   Manager   Personnel Department
                                                           Grievance Handler

(First Appeal Level)   Supervisor   Personnel Liaison for
                                                           Unit or Division

(Grievance)   Employee
                                       (Choice of alternate routes)

Submitting disputes to arbitration is a necessity if the parties are unable to agree in the grievance process. What must be guarded against in the arbitration situation is the creation of enmity between workers and supervision. The corporate attitude must be one of concern, and the primary objective must be justice. Thus the total atmosphere should be one of problem solving and not of personalities. In the grievance procedure, whenever possible, conflicts should be resolved through discussion of the issues rather than division into two armed camps. In arbitration the parties are involved in a win-lose struggle. The losing football team may be able to give a cheer to the victors, but in the workplace judgments as to who are winners or losers creates only enmity, distrust, and lowering of cooperation. If handled correctly and tactfully, however, the grievance procedure can play an effective part in resolving conflicts between employees and management, and effectively halt a major unionizing appeal.

Other Methods of
Handling Grievances

The grievance policy needs to be supplemented by other devices to provide employees with a more or less anonymous means for airing their personal complaints or grievances. Some of these are:

1. *Periodic employee meetings.* Small groups of employees meet periodically to voice discontents to members of management.

2. *The "open door" policy.* Widely proclaimed by management is the policy that any employee is free to talk to any member of management in order to voice grievances. In practice it rarely works.

3. *A board of neutrals.* Respected members of the community provide an outlet for arbitration purposes.

4. *Attitude surveys.* Periodic sampling of employee opinion is usually an effective and quantitative way to get a handle on employee dissatisfaction.

5. *Company grievance committee.* This committee is composed of department members, management members appointed by top management, and a member of management asked to serve by the grievant.

6. *An effective personnel department.* In order to function effectively in the grievance area, personnel must have the confidence of both employees and management, and be given time to talk to employees.

7. *A gripe box.* This approach provides an anonymous outlet, but due to its anonymity it is also ineffective.

8. *Training supervisors in grievance handling.* The man closest to the problems of employees should be trained in the prevention and handling of grievances.

All of these approaches have advantages and disadvantages. None is complete; a combination of programs will be needed. The emphasis, so far as the prevention of unionization is concerned, is to provide a vehicle for the expression of grievances. Expression, in many cases, is solution.

RESTRUCTURING THE ORGANIZATION

Studies in organization theory indicate that the structure of an organization directly affects creativity, motivation, interpersonal relationships, and a host of other parameters. The organizational structure sometimes has built-in defects which encourage workers to unionize. Thus the third area of strategy for management in its desire to eliminate the causes of unionization involves restructuring the organization to reduce built-in conflict. Some approaches in accomplishing this objective follow.

Reduce the Number of
Levels of Supervision

In many organizations the employee feels lost because he is so far removed from the decision makers who control his fate. Since both top management and the worker feel isolated, it is no wonder that communication problems occur.

Sears Roebuck is a good example of a relatively flat organization where there are only four levels of management between the president of the company and the salespeople in the stores. This type of organization forces management by objectives, since it increases the number of people reporting to a manager to a point where he cannot direct and control them in the conventional manner. Responsibility and authority have to be delegated. Usually the results are higher profits, better morale, and improved supervision.

Enlarge and Enrich Jobs

Enlarging the employee's job (which does not mean giving him more to do of what he is doing already) by giving him added responsibilities, and enriching the job by making additional assignments challenging, is an excellent way to build worker morale. Too often we have specialized jobs to the point where they are nothing more than mindless tasks (for example, auto assembly lines), and in the name of efficiency have denuded work of all meaning and creativity of expression. Non-Linear Systems, Texas Instruments, and other pioneering firms have experimented with non-assembly-line production and found that job enlargement and enrichment can actually increase production over assembly-line rates.

Build Integrated Work Teams

Interdepartmental squabbles are an interesting phenomenon in the industrial world. Rather than focusing on problem solving, units sometimes dissipate time and energy treating other units as "the enemy." This is a sign that specialization of functions (which has such disastrous effects on the individual worker) is adversely affecting unit objectives and producing a negative work atmosphere for employees.

Management should integrate units so that all functions which bear on the same problem are grouped together. Instead of splitting units by function:

AAA   BBB   CCC

they should be grouped to service the objective:

ABC   ABC   ABC

There are human relations benefits which accrue by way of increased communications, cooperation, and satisfaction. Needless to say, the employee who enjoys these things is not a union candidate.

This discussion represents only a general plan; the corporation needs to make the plan specific and effective if unionization is to be prevented. We should want to do these things (restructuring work, improving communications, delegating responsibility, and so forth) not because we fear the effects of a union, but because we have an interest in the individual employee and the development of the corporation. It is time that industry moved into the twentieth century in the area of human relations. As Douglas McGregor said in *The Human Side of Enterprise:*

I share the belief that we could realize substantial improvements in the effectiveness of industrial organizations during the next decade or two. Moreover, I believe the social sciences can contribute much to such developments. We are only now beginning to grasp the implications of the growing body of knowledge in these fields. But if this conviction is to become a reality instead of a pious hope, we will need to view the process much as we view the process of releasing the energy of the atom for constructive human ends—as a slow, costly, sometimes discouraging approach toward a goal which would seem to many to be quite unrealistic.

The ingenuity and perseverance of industrial management in the pursuit of economic ends have changed many scientific and technological dreams into commonplace realities. It is now becoming clear that the application of these same talents to the human side of enterprise will not only enhance substantially these materialistic achievements, but will bring us one step closer to the good society. Shall we get on with the job?

PART TWO

MANAGERIAL
EFFECTIVENESS

I met a traveller from an antique land
Who said: Two vast and trunkless legs of stone
Stand in the desert . . . Near them, on the sand,
Half sunk, a shattered visage lies, whose frown,
And wrinkled lip, and sneer of cold command,
Tell that its sculptor well those passions read
Which yet survive, stamped on these lifeless things,
The hand that mocked them, and the heart that fed:
And on the pedestal these words appear:
"My name is Ozymandias, king of kings:
Look on my works, ye Mighty, and despair!"
Nothing beside remains. Round the decay
Of that colossal wreck, boundless and bare
The lone and level sands stretch far away.
—*Percy Bysshe Shelley*

5

Are You Promotable?

At one time or another every employee in organization life has been concerned with the factors that affect his promotability and career advancement. From this career anxiety have stemmed questions like these: Where am I now? Where am I going? Where can I or where should I go in my career?

Out of the shadows surrounding these questions has emerged a mystique with numerous writers purporting to give the answers. You cannot pass a newsstand or a bookstore without seeing an array of publications on how to succeed in business. Many of these are based on the Protestant work ethic, which say that if we work hard, practice our craft diligently, and keep our nose to the grindstone, then one day we will be knighted Prince of the Pie-Filling Division. These career-planning manuals promise to give one the inside track to promotability in ten easy lessons. Generally those books and a token will get you a ride on the subway.

THE P'S OF PROMOTABILITY

If we define success as career mobility and vertical advancement, it is possible to identify some factors affecting career ascent. These promotability factors cannot be placed in any priority because different organizations, even within the same industry, accent different values and place different judgment weights on these indicators of management potential. And, again, departments within the larger organization tend to accentuate and underscore different values and characteristics. To an extent, the kind of fish caught depends on the lake in which you fish.

Promotability will vary also by function. Executives in personnel, research and development, manufacturing, and marketing tend to accentuate different dimensions and to give them different weights. And, everyone is well aware, one's own boss may accentuate different promotability criteria than the manager down the hall. But having accounted for the subtle differences, we have also noted the similarities and have identified these as the P's of promotability.

Performance

Very seldom can one get ahead without getting results on the job. As you look through the various levels of your organization's hierarchy, you find yourself wondering, "How did *he* ever make it?" One good look at the fellow's background—and he may be your boss—will show that he is and has been a performer, producing results rather than just activity. At least in this one regard the Protestant work ethic holds true: one must get results. One must produce and solve problems and make a contribution to get to the top of the career ladder. But performance is not the only factor, nor necessarily the prime factor, in the promotability formula.

Peer Acceptance

One of the reasons given for promoting a man is his acceptance by peers. This doesn't mean that the man who succeeds won a popularity contest, but he does have the respect and trust of his peers. He is an individual to whom others look for direction and guidance and for reliable information. The peer group looks to him for leadership. He earns the leadership role by setting values, giving purpose, and pointing the way in a committed, confident manner. Men who have the motivation or thrust to get a job done also tend to have a supportive constellation around them, a peer group that will pull with them rather than against them.

Politics

Politics is seldom discussed in the textbooks. Nor is it often covered in management courses. In most training programs, very little time, if any, is spent on this dimension that undergirds, facilitates, and oils the upward progress of the successful candidate. Playing politics has negative connotations. When we think of someone playing politics, we think of a person who plays dirty pool, who apple polishes—not to mention all the other polite and not so polite phrases that describe this kind of activity. We think of the politician as someone who is always in there with nice words to impress the boss, who finesses the executives to his own advantage.

But a form of politics that we have found to be genuinely useful to a man's career is the sense of being politic—that is, knowing when to interject ideas for change, knowing how to suggest the change, and being sensitive to the other power blocs in the situation. Politics was once defined as "the art of the possible." The man who is politic is a man who, through his own sensitivity, has psyched out his boss and his timely needs. He knows who has the political leverage and he knows when to talk to this person to get a decision. And while we may think that there is a stigma attached to politics, that there is something unclean or unpalatable in being a politician, we know from observation that managers who fail to establish the necessary political influence go nowhere.

Presentation of Self

A key personal characteristic of the ambitious manager is that he presents himself and his ideas with authentic impact. This does not mean that he is a phony or a role player or an actor. Rather, he is a real person who talks straight, knows what he stands for and what he stands against. He is worth listening to. With this self-knowledge, he presents himself and his ideas with some dramatic flavor and intensity. In other words, he stands out.

Problem Analysis

Analytical ability and creative thinking may have relatively little to do with a person's formal education. What we are talking about here is the ability to analyze a problem with insight. Persons who move ahead have a cognitive or intellectual component. Men who move ahead are not necessarily geniuses, but they are generally above the average measured intelligence. They have, if you will, above-average "smarts." They have the ability to go to the heart of the matter. This talent is a cognitive skill that is one of the prime reasons for their emergence from the group.

Pressure Handling

One of the questions a person asks himself when he is assessing his qualifications for a career in professional management is, "Can I hack the pressure?" Each one of us lives with pressure, anxiety, and tension. This pressure takes many forms and has many sources. Sometimes it revolves around our relationship to authority, sometimes it is anxiety about our obsolescence. Often it is free-floating. As we rise in the management hierarchy, the pressure increases. There is more long-term risk taking. You have less control over some of your predictions and the gambles you take than when you were on the research bench or at the accounting desk or on the manufacturing line close to the product itself.

If you don't have the stomach and nerves for pressure, then maybe you should not grab the brass ring on the promotion carousel, because it is very, very hard to let go once you have it. Your income has increased, your status in the community has gone up, and your family is beginning to outspend you at a higher level. Once your life style has changed and you have reached a higher level, to fail at that higher level tends to be quite traumatic. Simply speaking, do you have the "internal wiring" for stress?

One of the prime characteristics of the successful climber is his ability to handle pressure and to live with greater uncertainty. Look at yourself before you start to climb the management ladder. The trappings are fine—the money, the parking lot space near the door, the private secretary, the mahogany wastepaper basket, an occasional ride in the company plane. All these accoutrements and perquisites are lovely. However, the mental and physical consequences of failure are dramatic and sometimes catastrophic.

PERFORMANCE INDICATORS

Under the umbrella of the P's of performance, let's look at some of the subdimensions by studying the actual performance of a man who emerges and is nimble enough to survive as he climbs the management ladder. Without reciting that he is trustworthy, loyal, friendly, courteous, clean, brave, and reverent, and without regurgitating some of the nonsense that we find in the usual performance appraisals—the fact that his attendance is good, that he brushes his teeth, that he shines his shoes, and that he is a nice guy—let us focus on the indicators of performance that produce payoffs for both the organization and the man's career advancement.

Making Things Happen

The man who runs ahead in the corporate career race is a man who makes things happen. Despite obstacles, he has a competitive drive to see a job through to completion. He realizes that the test of executive excellence is how he reacts when life is going sour, when things are getting out of control, and when people are saying, "What are we going to do to get out of this mess?" When the pressure is highest and the problems are most difficult, these people go into high gear and function at their best.

These executives have the ability to make something significant happen. They do not confuse being busy with getting results. They seem to say to themselves, "What has to happen *now*? What must I do as an agent of change today in order to make something of significance happen tomorrow?" In turn, they commit themselves to action and accomplishment in terms of what *is* rather than what *should be* in the world around them.

Too many managers have a hang-up with the word "should." Should implies guilt if we fail, and it makes us run faster. It makes us uncomfortable. It makes us compulsive about detail, which in turn makes us lose sight of the big picture. Because of the anxiety "should" generates, we either run from it or we fight it by being busier and busier. We get worn out by running around in circles, but find that we actually accomplish very little. Some people spend their entire lives in industry, being very busy—and getting nowhere. The man who is going somewhere commits himself to action and accomplishment in terms of what is rather than what should be or might have been. His focus is here and now, on making things happen.

Critical Thinking and Problem Solving

The person who moves up has the ability to anticipate, to perform "cluster analysis" thinking; that is, he can correlate isolated events early and integrate them into an awareness that something is going wrong. He can identify patterns of scattered events that indicate a deviation from the set plan (which is the definition of a problem). There is a second factor in his ability to solve problems: he does his homework. It's no trick to know that you've got a *problem*. The winner is the manager who can present the *solution* by the time he goes to the boss's office with the problem. He knows what is meant by completed staff work.

Sensitivity

Part of the ability to critically analyze an organization comes from being tuned in to its informal life. Successful managers are sensitive to the informal world, as well as to the world of production around them. They get cues from various parts of the organization that something is going amiss, and then apparently integrate it into their work group. They have the ability to sift through related facts, decide which facts are significant, and pull them together to come up with an intelligent, practical applied plan.

There are many people in organization life who blow lots of steam, who impulsively go into the boss's office with false signals. However, when they are challenged they are unable to analyze what is happening. Or, if they understand what is happening, they have not thought it through and haven't been able to solve it.

Standing the Strain

Men who are mobile in their career can handle pressure. They tolerate stress and know how to wait out a situation. In other words, they don't have to have an immediate solution. They can live with an unsolved problem. Instead of focusing on speed, they take the time they need to consider alternatives and judge the consequences of each.

The higher one goes in management, the more ambiguity there is, the more uncertainty in the opinions that will be given to you. Can you live with it?

Here are some interesting questions to test yourself with: "How quickly do I need to have information certainty? How badly do I need definite structure in the organization world about me? How uncomfortable am I with ambiguity?"

Resiliency

A subdimension of stress handling is resiliency, the ability to bounce back from a defeat. What is your reaction when somebody says no in the organization system? Do you pout? Does it tear you up? Or can you get it out of your system and bounce back and go on from there? Can you say, "Well, this is life. I had my day in court. It's been a fair hearing, and the answer is no. Now I must go on without having other people hold my hand and not look for a lot of comfort from the organization womb." As you go higher in management, there will be fewer people around to hold your hand; instead there will be more and more visibility and exposure of one's errors. It's lonelier at the top than most people know.

Job Extension

People who move up in an organization are not satisfied with just performing the duties required in their job description. They tend to expand the limits of their jobs and find areas where their fellow employees are not covering a particular assignment or project. They are task grabbers who want more experience and more influence. They push the parameters and boundaries of their jobs to fit the needs of their own development and to meet the needs that they perceive as useful to the organization.

Another interesting facet of the job extender is that he is allowed to take on other duties because his boss trusts him. He has worked out a "psychological contract" with the boss in which the boss says, in effect, "Charlie, I know what you are doing, I know what you are up to. Just keep me wired in, keep me covered and I'll let you go ahead and do it because I trust you. I know that you are not undercutting me, that you are not going to embarrass me. I trust you because you are good. I trust you because I know that you want to do a good job." In other words, he builds a credit bank. Once his boss-credit is good, he is able to put himself in the posture, and to adopt the tactic, of job extension.

The individual who has not done his homework in terms of his relationship with his immediate boss will find that he has committed industrial suicide as far as job extension is concerned. The man's boss is going to be all over him when things go wrong. He is going to catch the man up short when he plays games in the job extension arena when those games do not have his psychological backing.

The job extender is curious and inquisitive. He is willing to view responsibility to the organization as an element that transcends his own job. He sees his job in relation to other jobs, looking outward and around, rather than myopically focusing on his own little world. He has a game plan for the needs of today, but he also has a path mapped out for his own development and for the development of the organization.

Giving It Away

The one factor that applies equally to all of us is time. There are only 24 hours a day to live and to make things happen. The question, therefore, is how to best allocate that time in order to achieve results, results on the job and results in our personal life. Not only does the emerging manager take on new assignments; he also delegates some of his present tasks to others in order to focus on the new opportunity.

People who move up are very conscious of time and are strict about how they use it. At your next coffee break try a survey of the men who work with you and ask them if they know to within 25 cents what their time is worth per hour. Many of them will need to work it out on paper because they do not know. But the pros, those who are involved in this serious business of furthering their careers, know what their time is worth.

Do you know where your time is going? Do you know the difference between wasting time and investing time? That is not just an idle phrase: the pro knows when he is investing his time. If a project has a low return for him, for his boss, or for his company, he doesn't get involved, because he knows it is going to cost him something. That seems rather crass, but in order for the man to make something happen, he often has to give away low-priority, time-consuming projects that compromise his ability to make things happen. He does not encumber himself with projects that eat up his time resource.

Timing

The effective manager is concerned about correct timing in making a proposal or suggestion. At the end of the day, rather than unloading all the problems on the boss, he runs a *perception check*. He says, "How's it been going?" And if his boss says, "It's been a rotten day," our bright young employee has the sense and the patience to wait. The ineffective employee, on the other hand, is so compulsive that he is unable to tolerate the anxiety of waiting, and so he charges in. Often the only difference between the "problem child"—the person who is a pain in the arm—and the person who is seen as the idea man is not in the quality of the ideas they present but in the timing of their presentation.

Cooperation and Conflict

Individuals who are aware of their responsibility to uphold the quality of organization living are also able to coordinate people effectively. They are able to coordinate situations from both the left side and the right. They are liaisons between work areas, between work projects; and because of job extension, they are able to take the different pieces and put the whole deal together. Therefore, they emerge as being slightly different from the rest of the work group. Because they have the ability and the courage, they are able to play an aggressive role, getting people to work together to make something happen.

The successful manager can make another person feel important. An acquaintance of ours has a unique hobby of collecting tombstone epitaphs. One that stands out in his mind reads: "He appreciated."

For organization living you must, in a very real sense, make the other person feel important. You must remind the other person that he is a somebody, rather than a nobody. The person who emerges in the career climb often generates an atmosphere that makes people feel better and more important when they are around him. People like to be around him because he is genuine and sensitive, which means that when he loves, he loves; when he respects, he respects; when he fights, he fights. He is not necessarily Mr. Popularity, but he has great credibility. Because of his honesty he can express disgust, anger, and disappointment as well as satisfaction and fulfillment. People know that a compliment from him is not just a hypocritical gesture toward "good human relations."

Good human relations stem from honestly being yourself, which enables others to know where they stand. In terms of organization living and personal relationships, we are speaking of a person of integrity. If you integrate your beliefs with your behavior, you will be authentic, "for real," and people will know it.

The successful manager also has the strength to confront conflict directly and accept differences in ideas. He is not necessarily a peace-maker, but neither does he run from interpersonal tension. He confronts himself; then he is able to confront others. He does it of course with tact and interpersonal diplomacy. But he does it! And he confronts in order to get results.

He is able to perceive the subtle relationships that exist around him. When these changes are detrimental to his boss or his organization or himself, he has the strength to confront them rather than gloss over them or hide from them. He is a competitor. He wants to win. Coach Woody Hayes of Ohio State University once said, "I am not a good loser because you have to lose to prove it." That is a statement of a man who wants to win. The emerging manager also wants to win; there is no question about it. We teach our children that it is not important whether they win or lose, but in industry if you don't play to win, forget it.

Sensitivity and Strengths

The sensitive executive tries to understand other people's viewpoints. He keeps an open mind and avoids making snap judgments. When something or someone is different from what he expected or wanted, he asks, "Why? What is occurring?" He doesn't label or sterotype people and events; he tries to understand them first. As a result, he doesn't short-circuit his own thinking or fallaciously come up with a conclusion that is going to make him look impulsive and embarrass himself and his boss. He is concerned with what is really happening.

What we are saying is that he is open in his group living. He lives comfortably and adequately within a group without alienating other people. He has peer acceptance and he stands out among others because he can deal with organizational perceptions. As a result he gets inside political information. He gets performance data. He gets sponsorship information that is not shared with his colleagues. He becomes eyes and ears for his boss and his organization. He is interested in what is going on in his group and concerned about protecting both the group and his boss. He is concerned about how the goal is going to be accomplished and about things that could go wrong in moving toward achievement of the goal.

But he does not do all this as a loner. He is not an independent contributor. Instead, he recognizes that he must integrate his knowledge and efforts with those of others. As a wise friend once observed, some men think they are giants. They simply do not realize that they are only pygmies, standing on the shoulders of giants. You cannot go up that ladder alone. Your ascension is based on an ability to coordinate the efforts and contributions of many other people. We indicated earlier the necessity of establishing a credit bank with the boss. The emerging manager has also developed a credit bank with his peers. He has developed an acceptance among them based on trust.

Part of a genuine relationship with others has to do with attitudes toward excellence. In areas where you excel, do not either deny or flaunt your excellence. And when you see strength and excellence in others, do not be frightened by it. Let the other person be strong where he is and you be strong where you are. In that way a sound relationship builds between the two of you.

The employee who moves ahead is respected by his associates. He draws ideas from other people without threatening them; he can interact with them without causing fear. The individual whom we have seen emerge in organizations does not seek grandstand credit and applause. He knows the limelight will find him when he has made his contribution. Because he understands the performance relationships that exist, because he works effectively within these subtleties and realities, he knows that the credit and applause which all of us would like to receive will eventually be his. Recognition comes to him, not he to recognition.

Development

Another dimension of the promotable manager is his willingness to surround himself with strong subordinates. He develops backups and replacements, and deliberately grooms employees who can replace him. He would rather have a swimming team of champions than a team of nonsinkers. Many people in management are concerned that someone may be after their job. They are insecure about this possibility and may remain so for the rest of their lives. This does not mean they are paranoid; it is one of the realities of organization life where there is high, personal competition and intensive dynamics resulting from group relations.

How does the manager handle this reality? Do you hire and surround yourself with people who can easily be controlled or do you surround yourself with talent? Are you, yourself, growing by having a strong backup? Are you able to talk about the strengths of your replacement? If you don't have anybody who will take your place, then you may be kept where you are. You are going to be damned by something that sounds good but will kill you in your career climb. You will become *indispensable*. Being indispensable is fine as far as ego is concerned, but it is the kiss of death for vertical career ascent. Supervisors who are moving vertically in their careers are able to develop other people to take their place. They are not concerned about keeping information from their strong backup people, but openly talk about the operational values and data that are involved in the immediate setting in which both of them work. They want employees to be highly effective. They want them to be as completely knowledgeable as possible when the time comes for them to step into the job.

A person's ability to rise to higher management has to do with what he has done for his own development. Higher management is impressed that he has a degree, and they appreciate that he ran certain profit centers in the company five years ago. But what has he done for the company lately; and what has he done for himself? Where has he appreciated in value—becoming stronger, more capable, and more of a pro? Some employees, in the absence of any formal organization program, will develop their own. Some will take advantage of courses offered at the local university or will engage in community activities to increase their leadership ability. They will in some manner commit themselves to an active, planned program that will strengthen their abilities. The employee who will emerge is aware that he must continuously grow just to survive. While you read this book as part of your own development program, some of your would-be competition are home watching television.

Identification with Management

It is not uncommon to hear a new supervisor or manager say, "They want us to do something"; or "They have interpreted the policy to mean"; or "They said. . . ." The emphasis is on the pronoun *they* as opposed to the pronoun *we*. When one joins the management of a company, he is entrusted by the owners of a company, the stockholders, with the hard dollars and cents they have invested in that corporation. There are jobs on the payroll because the owners feel they need this much effort. Managership is not just a title, it is a trusteeship.

Unfortunately, some managers and supervisors still see themselves as employees. Their primary concern seems to be how they can slip out to a convention or sneak off from work. Somehow the organization is considered to be a self-interest-fulfilling vehicle. It is natural to be concerned about our own interests. A big *I* operates inside us all. The question is, does the big *I* exploit opportunities and consider itself to have priority over the managership of the resources that have been committed to its trust?

Do you identify with the real profit-and-loss situations that your company faces? The number of managers who have little regard for the costs they generate is amazing. Observe in your own organization the competition to keep ahead of Jones down the hall, who just requisitioned an electronic calculator. Now everyone has to have one. The costly nonsense that goes on in playing the status game reflects a basic disregard for the reason a manager is given his position.

The person who emerges (for his own reasons and for the welfare of his company) tends to care about what return the company gets on the investment it has put into the area he operates. He identifies with the management process, and his goals coincide with those of corporate management.

Do you see your problems as being interlocked with those of your boss? When your boss has made commitments, do these become your commitments? The employee who emerges tends to think, "When my boss makes a commitment, it is my commitment, on a win, lose, or draw basis." This does not mean he rubberstamps the decision. He may be very concerned about possible negative implications, and he may argue with his boss about it in private. But when he comes out of the boss's office it becomes a joint commitment.

One of the most remarkable boss-subordinate relationships that we ever observed was between a vice president of manufacturing and the director of operations, who was his immediate subordinate. When people from other areas or within his area came to the vice president with a proposal, he would ask for a presentation. He would then ask his director to play the role of devil's advocate or to make his own opposing feelings known. After a debate over the relative merits of the case, the vice president would make his decision. When that decision went against a position taken by the director, the director's immediate response was to firmly follow through to make sure that the vice president's decision was implemented. He was not a yes man nor a weakling who was afraid to take on an issue or a personality. He was a very effective, forceful presenter of his own ideas. But when his boss made a commitment, then the time for talking and debating was over. That commitment, whether he liked it or not, became a decision to which he firmly committed himself. His follow-through was based on an attitude that said "*We* want," not "*He* wants."

These, then, are some of the characteristics we have noted in persons moving into the ranks of management. They reflect a substantial change in organizational values and a shift in emphasis from the technology and techniques of management to what Douglas MacGregor called "the human side of enterprise."

6

What Do Effective Managers Do?

In recent years American industry has been caught in an increasingly tighter profit squeeze. International competition has increased and government regulation has intensified. Today one of the key factors in industrial survival is the maximization of managerial and organizational effectiveness. Some organizations have tried to stem the tide by selecting uncommon people. They have launched intensive recruiting campaigns to secure the best new talent available from business and other schools, as well as trying to obtain seasoned executives, engineers, and marketing men. Although it is important to have such talent on board, emphasis on finding the uncommon man seems to overshadow management responsibility to develop their present people to become more effective.

In terms of earnings and career mobility, the hard reality is that one of the things that separates the person who is going somewhere in management from the one who isn't is the degree to which he understands and uses the principles that produce results. The first duty of being a manager, superintendent, or first-line supervisor is to get effective results, not activity. Industry is not interested in frantic activity and fevered rushing to and fro. It wants predictable results. The executive who gets results has the ability to get effective contributions from his subordinates.

ON BEING EFFECTIVE AND EFFICIENT

Everyone in management has an array of resources at his disposal. The question is, how will he use them? Everything the man in management does, or everything he wants to do, hinges on his ability to get others to perform. We have found that many managers, supervisors, and vice presidents believe that their efforts should be focused on *maintaining* the organization. They are preoccupied with efficiency.

If you were to ask a group of managers what it is that they do, somewhere in their description will be the statement, "I solve problems." Of course they have problems, but is the manager's prime calling and responsibility to solve problems? It is not. He is to delegate that job. The manager's job is to focus his attention on the opportunities that surround him.

Managers spend too much time working on problems rather than letting their people solve the problems. Managers' work should lend itself to impact, significant achievement, and results. Too often in industry there is activity rather than significant change—the result of the fundamental confusion between being efficient and being effective.

In his book, *The Effective Executive,* Drucker points out that efficiency is *doing things right.* Effectiveness, on the other hand, is *doing the right things.* There is nothing so useless as doing with great efficiency what should not be done at all. We all know a Charlie who fills out all the forms just right and follows the procedure manual down to the last detail. But we also notice that he isn't promoted. We can't really blame Charlie, because we have all been taught to be neat and tidy, that anything worth doing is worth doing right. But that old maxim is less true than it seems, and has led many people into a lamentable waste of time. Many things that are worth doing with a *little* time and effort are not worth doing if they require a lot of time and effort. Time is a measure of life, and every kind of work ought to be adjusted to it. One of the commonest mistakes we all make is spending ourselves on things whose value is below the value of the time they require.

WHOSE PRIORITIES?

The management reality is that what is right to do largely depends upon what will give real results. Rightness is concerned with timing; it is the determination of what needs to be done for significant contribution now. The successful manager asks himself, What job needs to be done today? This week? What can I do as a leader that will significantly improve the effective contribution of my area? What does my customer need? If he is efficient he says, What can I do to meet my goals, my needs; what must I do to solve my problems? If he is effective, he says, What can I do to help my customer down the hall to do his job better? The effective manager has learned that he must perceive beyond his own group.

One of the frightening signs we have seen in dying organizations—whether a work group, a division, or a whole company—is that they are focused on their own internal priorities. They have not learned that their purpose is *to serve others*. The dynamic organization focuses attention *outward*, with priorities set in terms of the customers' needs. It exists to facilitate the happening of things in other people's areas. This attitude makes all the difference in the business world.

What can be done to move toward effectiveness? The first thing is to open up the communication channels. You can identify your real objectives by determining what your boss's problems and his boss's opportunities are. If you perform these analyses continually, recognizing that time changes priorities, then the battle is half won.

The other half of that battle is to concentrate on getting rid of all the trivial demands on your time and attention. The effective manager eliminates the nonessentials. He gives away the marginal activities because he knows that they cost him the most valuable resource that he has—his time. He also knows that they can cost him his career.

THE USE OF POWER

As conventionally defined, management is a process of getting things done through the efforts of other people. In order to get things done through others, the mature manager knows that he must use his influence to help others create, maintain, and attain job objectives. He has to be able to use his power to remove obstacles so that others can perform.

A common complaint of supervisors is that they've been given tremendous responsibilities without adequate authority to achieve results. This theme is heard not only at the first-line level, but all the way up the management ladder. One of the distinguishing characteristics of the person who moves out and stays in front is that he is not afraid to use power. He has learned how to use whatever influence is at his disposal to get things done.

Successful men seldom use their formal authority to make things happen. Rather they rely on the informal world of interpersonal relationships to accomplish their objectives. They know that the organization chart does not reflect the real sociological patterns of influence.

Interpersonal skill can be illustrated by comparing these hypothetical phone conversations. In the first call a recently promoted manager dials the head of purchasing. He says, "Mr. Smith, this is Mr. Klutz. I'm the new manager of veeblefesters; you've probably seen the announcement of my promotion in your new organization chart. I need this, that, and the other for my unit and I would like you to get them for me as soon as possible. I'll pick them up at 11:30 next Wednesday."

Mr. Smith, head of purchasing, replies, "Yes, I did see that you had been recently promoted. Congratulations and best wishes. I'm certain we in purchasing can be of service to you. If you'll be so kind as to fill out Form No. 11-00-11-38 in quadruplicate and have your boss's boss sign it, we'll be glad to put the paperwork through for you. We should be able to get those items easily in the next 90 days." "But," says the new manager, "I need it within the next few days." Says the head of purchasing, "I'm sorry, but that is the written procedure that must be followed." And so our new manager, while crisply efficient, was grossly ineffective. He pulled rank, made demands, and got nothing for his efforts. He is already failing in his job relations.

In another area of the company, Mr. Bogart, also a new manager, calls purchasing. His conversation goes like this: "Hey, Charlie, how are you doing? Great to hear your voice. I saw you out at the lake last weekend fishing. Did you catch anything?" They have about a five-minute discussion on fishing, how the kids are, et cetera, et cetera. Finally he gets down to the matter of business: "Say, do you have anybody who could help me get this, that, and the other? I'm really in a bind and could use them within the next few days. I sure could use your help on this one." "No sweat," says the head of purchasing. "When I'm out for coffee I'll pick them up for you." "Gee," says the new manager, "I'd sure appreciate it, but you don't have to go to that bother." Smith says, "No bother at all, but you know we have all these forms you have to fill out that are a real pain in the neck. I'll get you the parts you need, but make sure I'm covered by having someone run the forms through the system as quickly as possible." And our new manager responds, "That's the least I can do. I sure appreciate the favor and won't forget it."

The lesson is self-evident. Some managers do not understand that their power is not for themselves and for their own preservation. Interpersonal skill is important, but its purpose is to assist other people in getting their job done. The key question is, "Am I a power pump, a power facilitator, or am I a power inhibitor, a power bottleneck?" You need to use your power and your influence to assist other people in getting their job done and to push something through the system. The immature manager uses power to feed his own ego needs. You can consistently keep people in their place or you can use your domination to reduce people to less than they are. Every person in management has the ability to use his power to roll stones out of the way for the other person or to place them in his path. The effective manager knows that his power has been given to him to be used to help other people get their jobs done.

RESULTS THROUGH
THE EFFORTS OF OTHERS

All of us tend to want to do things ourselves rather than manage others and get them to do what they should. To resist this tendency, continue to ask yourself the action question, "Am I doing anything that the people reporting to me or available staff services *can do, should do,* or can be *trained to do*?" If the answer is yes, then you are failing yourself and your company. If the answer is no, you are in a position to do the important things—the tasks of managing.

Other guiding questions are on the instructive side: What projects, objectives, and needs for achievement should I work toward now? What priorities am I going to set, in what directions am I going to move, how am I going to use my skill today so that something significant happens, rather than just maintaining the shop as it was maintained last week? By keeping your eye on those questions you will be more likely to remember that the important is seldom urgent, and the urgent is seldom important. The corollary of that statement is that as a manager you delegate the urgent and keep the important. The urgent is delegated to your "pros"; you are paid to do the important work of planning, organizing, reviewing, and facilitating.

When that urgent request comes in, the developing manager goes to the employee on his staff who is the most knowledgeable and most effective person to handle that kind of situation.

The manager's job is to know this man and to know how to use him. The manager keeps for himself the important activities of planning, controlling, influencing, and directing. He is being paid to be a specialist in managing. Some people confuse the issue by saying that management men are generalists, but they are really specialists in management, and part of that specialization is knowing how to match the urgent problems to the right subordinate talents.

The effective manager learns how to juggle the interests and balance the demands from other departments for his organization's activities. He reconciles the interests of these beneficiaries so that he can serve them all. It is precisely because he is accountable to many interest groups that he has learned to mediate among the various interested parties to insure that each gets its share of the outputs of his organization. To get effective results he continually sets and resets priorities on high payoff projects. He balances the use of his resources; he is continually trying to optimize results through the effective use of men, machines, materials, money, minutes, mission, and methods—the resources at his command.

The focus for the effective manager is on what needs to be done, on what can be improved. He must know how matters stand at all times and what should be abandoned or delegated. His focus is on the end result—the objectives. He knows that he must produce and he has learned that the key to achieving objectives lies in getting commitments from his management, his peers, and his employees.

We underscore the importance and difficulty in formulating and communicating precise, understandable targets. Perhaps the greatest value of management by objectives is that it aids the commitment process by clearly defining the standards of performance, the responsibility levels, and the authority inherent in each performance task. Differences usually exist between a man and his boss as to what the man is supposed to do. And it is this lack of agreement that causes misunderstanding, confusion, and failure to reach objectives in the interpersonal unhappiness accompanying these misperceptions and falling short of target.

GUIDELINES FOR EFFECTIVENESS

The following suggestions are offered as guidelines to the manager who desires to increase his interpersonal effectiveness:

1. Keep all communications simple and straightforward. Limit written communications where possible (don't be an efficient, time-wasting memo writer); when a communication must be in written form, keep it pointedly short. Put your recommendations and request for action on page one; don't make the reader search for them.

2. Once you have made a decision on an issue, set up control procedures that allow you to follow through. Set a date for review of activity and then keep pace with that commitment by checking to make sure that all work has been carried out. Do not pass over a date of progress control on your calendar.

3. Capitalize on the strengths of people and learn to make allowances for their weaknesses. Do not try to change personalities by playing the role of amateur psychotherapist. Your concern is what a man can do for you now, what strengths he has that you can build on.

4. Remember that *everybody's* responsibility is *nobody's* responsibility. When you make an assignment, be clear about who must carry the ball. For maximum motivational impact, it is best to assign the task to one person rather than to an entire group.

5. Do not be afraid to exercise your leadership role. A lot has been written about participative management, and we recommend it heartily. But do not abdicate your decision-making prerogatives. It is up to you to provide the direction, the purpose, and the challenge for excellence.

6.   In interpersonal communications with more than one person, try to communicate to the group as a whole rather than through chain communication. Executive-to-group communication is not only a better use of your time, but questions from one member of the group may clarify the issue for all the other members. Don't let rumor distort your ideas and intentions.

SUPERVISORY CLIMATE CONDITIONS

The effective manager seeks to establish an atmosphere in which his employees can be properly oriented and motivated toward task accomplishment. The effective manager treats his personnel as though they are effective. His attitude implies that he assumes they will perform effectively. He communicates his high regard for them and his high expectations of them. And it is because he has high expectations that he asks them to commit themselves. The motivational impact on people who work for such a leader has been demonstrated time and time again. It is the executive who demands much that gets much. Treat your employees like pros. Expect them to behave accordingly.

The manager enhances this climate for achievement by giving his people freedom to make decisions and to make mistakes. He gives them real responsibility and the authority necessary to carry out that responsibility. He enlarges and enriches the man's job by making him think.

He is honest in his relation with the staff personnel on his team. He trusts them and supports them. This support is not only in an emotional sense, but also by supplying the necessary logistics for achieving results. The manager facilitates task accomplishment by utilizing his power to back his people.

He establishes clear, challenging goals. The entire environment is goal oriented. Members of the team thus come to think in terms of setting objectives and accomplishing them. Things really happen when you expect them to.

Employees need to influence the enterprise through their manager, and management should listen to what they have to say. Consultative managers make fewer assumptions and ask more questions. Because management is receptive to information input and feelings, members of the team are motivated to contribute their knowledge and their suggestions. This communication is further enhanced by management giving feedback to employees on a regular basis. The performance appraisal should not be considered a chore, but rather an opportunity to expand mutual understanding.

The successful manager has learned to respect the individual differences and strengths of his employees and to distribute assignments accordingly. He understands that it is important for them to have successful experiences and to use their talents. He does not assign tasks beyond their ability, but he involves them in tasks that stretch their level of competence. He further expects and encourages self-renewal and growth by placing the emphasis on development through *doing*. He is not content and will not let his staff be content to do tomorrow's job with yesterday's level of skill.

In a good climate the manager and employees function as a team. He acknowledges that he has a responsibility for their success as individuals. He does not let a person feel that he has been abandoned or that no one is interested in the success of his project.

At meaningful stages in a project's development, regular critical sessions are held. Questions to evaluate effectiveness and needed logistic support are asked: "What did we say we were going to do? What did we do? How could we do it better next time? What did we learn?" The emphasis is on help and evaluation to insure greater probability of future task accomplishment.

Because he is concerned with results, he communicates the expected results and the standards of performance. And once the assignment is given, he does not back seat drive, he does not coach over the shoulder, he does not kibitz, but instead lets the staff expert do the job on his own initiative. It may not be the way the manager would have done it, but it is being done the way the specialist in the ranks wants to do it. The manager knows that he still has control, and if results do not measure up, the employee will receive the appropriate performance evaluation. But the manager does not try to predetermine the means to the ends or stick his spoon in the pie.

When problems arise or results are less than expected, the mature manager does not resort to badgering his subordinates. He is not personality centered but problem centered. His approach is to discuss why the project fell short of the mark and to determine what corrective action can now be taken. Because of his desire to achieve results, even if backtracking is necessary, the manager will not deliberately alienate those who will in the final analysis enable him to achieve the objective.

The manager who succeeds and who stays out in front of his competition does not confuse efficiency with effectiveness. His focus is on task accomplishment by proper use of resources at his disposal, primarily the human resource. He so structures and challenges that human resource toward reaching the goal that the contributions made by his unit are distinguished by their innovation and their meaningfulness. In the process, employee development occurs, jobs are enriched, and organizational and self-renewal take place.

7

The Operating Manager's Accountabilities

Managership carries with it a wide range of responsibilities that seldom appear in the job description. To a large measure, these formal and informal responsibilities determine management effectiveness or failure. Let's discuss these unwritten accountabilities to find out why.

COMMUNICATION

Communication is imperative to lessen both individual and group anxieties. When managerial communications fail to circulate, corporate communication arteriosclerosis results, resulting in minimal significant information flow.

As a middle man in idea traffic and a prime mover in interactions, the manager can facilitate or block the flow of ideas. It is his responsibility to be an active solicitor of ideas and a transmitter of values, not simply a passive go-between. He promotes the flow of ideas, needs, and feelings between the executive culture and the subordinate culture. The executive culture has its values, needs, mores, and different ways of perceiving just as the subordinate culture does. The manager must act as a key link between these two cultures.

Effective communication requires sensors—attuned, sensitive people who should be placed throughout the organization. They must recognize vital information, that is, information the manager needs for his organization's success. A manager who gives the impression that he is only a collector of information will receive only distorted and limited information. But by developing and educating individuals throughout the organization and teaching them what they ought to be attuned to, he has a higher probability of getting vital information.

Communicating for Political Visibility

The manager is the prime agent for intra- and intergroup communication—the prime channel for communicating the group's activities, needs, and accomplishments. It is his responsibility to gain recognition and stature for his group, particularly for its high-producing individuals. Some departments seem to function in a corner. When this happens, people begin to ask, "What does that group do?" or, "Is that department still with us?" This is a striking case of a manager's communication failure. He spent more time communicating downward to his subordinates than in communicating the services and contributions of his group upward and outward to other managers.

Some units fail to get their budget requests approved because a manager has not laid the appropriate groundwork. If higher management does not know what the group is contributing there may be no extra budget allocations. Effective managers do not wait until a month before budget proposal time to start talking about their group's contributions; such information should be periodically communicated upward.

What, specifically, needs to be communicated?

Department goals and achievements. Often top management people forget what a certain group is doing; they aren't aware of the worth and mission of the group anymore. It is the manager's responsibility to communicate the goals and any extraordinary accomplishments of his group and to keep them in higher management's eye.

Employee attitudes. Many times management chooses only to communicate data. When employees are restless or dissatisfied or when they are happy or enthusiastic, it is important to communicate such feelings to higher management.

Needs, problems, and growth opportunities. The manager who only tells his superiors about all the things that are running smoothly ("We don't have a need in the world, we don't have any operating problems") is either deluding himself or trying to delude management. It is important to focus higher management's attention on the group's problems and needs as well as on the barriers that prevent a group's accomplishing its objectives, and those opportunities that can produce results.

Communication with Employees

What do employees want to know? The manager should communicate to them the broad view of why they are engaged in their activities—the personal and organizational rationale for task performance. Subordinates are interested in knowing the impact on, and the relevant contribution of their activities to, the total system. They want to know the needs of higher management; perhaps they have heard rumors about topside problems and such rumors become increasingly distorted. Rumor can be your enemy. Thus a manager does well to communicate truthfully the needs of and the threats to the company.

Knowing about problems will also enable the employees to help. Perhaps they will come up with suggestions to correct the situation. In addition, when a manager communicates these concerns to employees there is the side benefit of increased identification and cohesiveness with the company. Employees want to identify with the enterprise and to know their jobs are meaningful. When people are asked for suggestions it then becomes "our" problem, not "their" problem topside, and group solidification can result.

Employees want and need to know many things: the impact of their contributions, organization problems, management's feelings, and the actual business changes of the company. People like to be proud of where they work. They like to know when the company is succeeding and what its new projects and future plans are. When management deprives employees of this type of information, the "we" feeling suffers; management secrecy causes employees to feel they are being treated like children. Adult feelings are the result of being talked to as an adult.

Applied Communication

Below are some principles that may be helpful in making a proposal to your executives and getting it approved. The overall objective is to get the idea accepted or into the approval pipeline for decision. Many fail at this first stage; they get the idea as far as their own boss, but it never gets to a higher level of approval.

1. Word the proposal in terms of the executives' frame of reference. Self-centered presentations usually fail because they are not presented with the boss's point of view in mind or do not take into account his needs, fears, concepts, and background. Whether it is a formal chart presentation, verbal discussion, or memo, the communicator must put his idea into language that the listener understands.

2. Set the stage by providing supporting documents. Many a manager or staff man has created a workable proposal but lost out because he

didn't do his homework. Do not catch the listener cold. Provide him with backup information ahead of time to assist him in his decision making. On the other hand, don't give him a 30-page razzle-dazzle proposal. He hasn't got time to read it, much less comprehend it.

Where the executive might have questions or doubts, provide an appendix of supporting information anticipating his questions. It is unlikely you will succeed if your boss feels he is afraid of the newness of your idea or that he doesn't fully understand the idea.

However, by giving him the supporting data that will lead him to logical conclusions and recommendations, he will appear knowledgeable; he can appear to be the expert, not only in his boss's eyes but in yours as well. *Let your boss be the hero.* Ask yourself what he really needs to know to act upon the proposal, what emotional or ego support he needs, and give it to him. Without it the reactions will be indecision, rejection, or a frustrating request for more facts.

3. The communication itself should be brief, direct, simple, and relevant and should *request action.* Higher managers will want to know what is expected of them. If the sender hasn't told them, it is just a piece of paper. Your information must be relevant; too many men devote paragraph after paragraph to irrelevant data, leading the reader through 18 pages before arriving at the conclusion. Put your conclusion and request for the action in the first part of the document.

4. Provide the return on investment "we" can expect from your proposal to support your boss in making his proposal to higher management. If you don't state anticipated results and payoff, you will be doing a disservice to your idea and to your boss. Ask yourself what your boss's boss needs to know and how your boss communicates with his boss. By incorporating this sensitivity into your writing, by providing operating objectives, you will help the proposal move along through the approval system.

5. The effective manager integrates his information so that the receiver can draw clear, appropriate conclusions. Often an executive is at a disadvantage, having less information than his subordinate. You must be able to guide your manager to the right conclusion; lead him to the honest conclusions which call for action, attention, and decision. After your boss is through reviewing the presentation, he should not have to ask, "What does he want me to do? What conclusion should I draw?"

6. Provide alternatives for action and estimate the probability of risk in these alternatives. Many a manager has succeeded because he has built his initial recommendation on solid grounds and because he has provided first and second alternatives to his proposal with the risks and consequences clearly identified.

DECISION MAKING

Action is the manager's primary reason for being. His responsibility is to turn information—his own ideas and those of his staff—into action. Management's worst enemy is indecision. Decision-making authority separates the manager's role from his subordinate's.

Decision skill and personal courage further separate the successful manager from the unsuccessful one. A manager is paid for the relevance and competence of his decisions. The company put him in his position because it feels he has the potential to make sound return-on-investment decisions. The skill to make such decisions is based on his ability to solicit the necessary information on existing needs and forecast opportunities.

There is a distinct separation between the manager who tries to run things by a let's-vote operation and the participating manager. The latter solicits predictive information, encouraging his people to forecast opportunities as well as potential problems, and to offer alternative solutions. However, the participating manager still makes the final decision. In the last analysis, decisions are the prerogative of the manager. He is the one who will be held accountable: "the buck stops here."

One of the hallmarks of quality decision making is to balance employee involvement and a manager's formal authority. One of management's great challenges is to achieve this subtle balance, to be able to capitalize on the ideas that employees present, thus giving them confidence in their manager, while at the same time using decision authority to direct those employees. A manager needs to balance his personal decisions with the participating contributions of his group. Your subordinates must feel that you genuinely want their suggestions; they will trust and respect you and will become involved in your objectives if you try to balance their ideas with your final authority to decide the best course of action.

Management decisions should reflect those areas that offer the greatest promise of progress. Managers, for the most part, are judged on their number of decision wins. Higher management will tolerate some mistakes, but you need to have enough decisions on the winning side of the ledger.

Decisions must also be politically viable. Decisions and proposed tasks need political support. We are not referring to playing office politics but to being politic, that is, judicious. A politic decision is one calculated and timed to succeed where there is a real possibility of success. Decisions, before they can be turned into action, must have political life. If the decision is in an area that is not possible politically, the manager is asking for barriers to his proposals right from the start. Politic decision making is the art of the possible in terms of the climate, resources, and mind-set of the powers that be.

Decisions must facilitate the flow of achievement. Something must happen as the result of a management decision. Any time a decision is delayed, rechanneled, or restudied, the manager must ask himself whether he is acting as a bottleneck or a pump. The effective manager makes sure that ideas flow and that the work moves on as a result of his decision.

Decisions must mesh short-range accomplishment with long-range objectives. Concentrate on the plans of higher management, and mesh your short-range objectives with the long-range program.

Decisions must be focused on opportunities. Some decision makers are fire fighters, constantly focusing on crises. The only time they make a decision is when they are faced with a problem. If you see an opportunity, if you can create an opportunity, make a decision in those areas that lead to innovative return on investment.

Barriers to Decision Making

Three general factors complicate managerial decisions. First, a manager makes his decision in an extended time frame as opposed to the day-to-day decisions of a foreman. The higher one goes in management, the longer the time lapse for the decision to have results. For example, a president of a company makes decisions that will affect the company for five, ten, or twenty years, or even longer.

The second factor is that many times the decisions are outside the manager's area of technical expertise or formal training. He finds himself supervising an array of different backgrounds and professional disciplines. The manager has one of two choices: He can try to be an expert in many different areas or he can accept his place as a manager and not try to be the expert's expert. His subordinates want the manager to make decisions based on logic, critical thinking, executive top-side knowledge, and human relations skills. They no longer expect him to be the technical expert. *They* are the pros.

This may be difficult for a new manager to realize and accept. A person who moves from the technical operation into the managerial ranks may suffer "separation anxiety." Now he has to make decisions beyond his own expertise, taking risks and chances. He has to know his people and the quality of information they are giving him. His key is to hire and manage experts, and learn to rely on their advice.

A third factor is that a manager must make decisions in gray areas. Such decisions place managers in the realm of ambiguity. The higher a manager goes in the hierarchy, the more ambiguity anxiety he experiences because there are fewer tangibles. Executive decisions involve emotional risk taking in view of the necessarily limited and abstract long-range information he must work with.

Addressing the Decision

Faced with these obstacles, how can a manager reach sound decisions? The first requirement is to develop a skill for calling upon other people's talents and perceptiveness. A successful manager must know where the talent is and how to capitalize on it.

A manager must also know how to ask clear questions and elicit information. He counts heavily on his critical evaluation skill so that he can separate the relevant from the irrelevant, the biased from the unbiased.

Managerial decision making also includes eliminating services and processes that have outgrown their usefulness. Perhaps these services were appropriate and effective at one time, but the very essence of organization living is change, and the effective manager knows when to change.

Another ingredient of management decision making is creating new priorities. Part of a manager's job is salesmanship—selling the new ideas of his department to other departments. Where a manager can create new priority projects he makes decisions there. You must stay flexible in moving, shifting, and recalibrating your operating priorities.

A manager must have the courage to take action, the courage to act even if it means running the risk of making some mistakes. Commitment to choose in a context of ambiguity is like Kierkegaard's leap into the abyss; it is a sign of faith in the rightness of our perceptions. The commitment and accountability to choose are yours.

RELATIONSHIPS

A manager has the privilege, challenge, and responsibility to manage events in terms of their anticipated human relations impact. Very few managers fail because of technical incompetence. Instead, they fail in their relations with their boss, their subordinates, or their peers. The manager's world rests on building and sustaining interpersonal relations.

The manager must take the time to identify the job-related and personal needs of others. He must ask himself how different personality needs dovetail with the ability to accomplish different jobs that need to get done and with the needs of the organization. Effectiveness in organization life depends on aligning the needs of the organization with the needs of the individuals who work for it. If managers assign tasks with individuals' needs in mind, organizations will have more job-satisfied employees, more enriching, meaningful jobs, and a higher level of productivity and quality.

A manager's task is to foster the freedom of his people—not to demand conformity. He must also understand that people would like fulfillment in their jobs, not just a place to work. Most individuals have a desire for freedom of movement, self-choice, and task input. Management's responsibilities are to encourage employees to *be,* to *belong,* and to *become.* Employees want the freedom to be themselves, to belong, and to become, and to achieve by searching for fulfillment through task breadth.

A manager capitalizes upon the needs of his staff. Show an individual, when you give him a work assignment, how he can get some personal reward from his assignment—where he can be a person in his own right or where he can become something as a result of his assignment. Present and describe the assignment in terms of your subordinate's personality so he can see some psychological payoff and job growth.

The Courage to Be Courageous

In your relations with subordinates urge them to be as courageous as possible. If you inculcate the fear of doing anything wrong by treating them like children, the results will be literalism and strict adherence. Instead, encourage your employees to be strong, to take risks, and to explore for knowledge. Managers don't build a strong team by having obedient employees. If a manager maintains a team of "weak sisters," there is a probability that he will not be going anywhere himself since his own management may see him as indispensable to his current job.

Whatever task behavior is desired, support it; this is one of the basic principles of learning. Whenever desirable behavior occurs, reinforce it with recognition. Many executives have difficulty expressing praise. Yet praise, recognition, attention, concern, and interest are at the disposal of the mature manager. By encouraging employees to do their own thinking, they will pride themselves on their ability to evaluate and predict, and they will gain an opportunity for further self-development.

Another part of a manager's job is to provide meaningfulness within the work itself. If the job does not contribute anything, remove it. On the other hand, if an employee does not realize the meaningfulness and importance in his work, communicate that meaningfulness to him. Management is responsible for making every job assignment relevant, because, in itself, it has no intrinsic meaningfulness. Meaningfulness is extrinsic rather than intrinsic to a job. Because employees need to identify with the total work flow and to know the effect of their efforts, let them know the purpose of their job. Job enrichment is not job enlargement; job enrichment is making and restructuring the job content relevant to the employee who is doing that job.

Environment of Trust

Another part of managerial responsibility is to create an achieving atmosphere conducive to accomplishment. The work climate is directly related to one's immediate manager and indirectly related to the management hierarchy all the way to the president's office. What the manager should project into that environment is mutual trust. An environment of human ecology that encourages, supports, and reinforces an individual's self-worth adds immeasurably to this mutual trust. A manager must communicate by looks, actions, and words his honest and high regard for his people. An ecosystem of emotional security allows people to try; it provides an opportunity to express themselves without fear of reprisal. To create this human ecology environment of trust, communicate sincere feelings to others. By emotionally leveling with his employees, a manager can help them appreciate that he is human too. This sounds elementary, yet it is a principle that is often violated. Some managers feel they have to be superior in their subordinates' eyes; if they don't appear to be strong or powerful they won't command respect. Such a manager cannot relate to his people for fear that they might recognize his shortcomings. Some of the most successful, emotionally mature managers are those who can admit what they don't know and ask for others' opinions. The more you are able to level with your people, the more they will trust you, because they know you first as a human being and second as a manager.

Provide Success Experiences

Provide opportunities for people to enjoy psychological success, particularly the new employee. We all need to have the step-by-step experience of evolving success. Giving an overwhelming assignment to a new man right off the bat can cause a high probability of failure. To build a good relations climate, start a new employee with an assignment that has a high probability of success. He will then be able to develop self-confidence as you give him bigger and bigger assignments, increasing risk little by little. All the time the man receives a personal payoff through success experiences. Thus a manager strengthens both his relationship with the employee and the employee's identification with the job.

Effective working relations are built on a feeling of essentialness, a sense of contribution. People have to feel important and need to be needed. A man has to feel he is essential to an operation and is a meaningful contributor to the overall welfare and progress of the project. Show him why he is essential, why he is meaningful to you and the unit. Job death is just another phrase for not being needed. Provide a sense of confirmation, a feeling of self-affirmation. The more a manager can encourage and reinforce, the more he can create a good relations climate, one that will produce results through caring and pride.

Employee Participation

When employees have had a hand in planning what is to be accomplished they know what to expect. When a manager keeps his people guessing, results will be poor. If people can predict events, if they don't have to take punitive risks to find out, if they know the ground rules and participate in planning, the relations climate will be enriched.

Relations are further enhanced by the acceptance of innovation and *idea* nonconformity (we are not speaking of nonconformist behavior). Idea nonconformity and innovation have their place and a manager needs to promote them, encourage them, use them, and reward them. The more he squelches this kind of growth, the more people will lose their self-esteem and their task motivation. Relations will suffer and will produce on-the-job retirement.

Relations improve when people feel they have stature and personal dignity. Many a manager feels he gains strength by playing down the dignity of an individual, by straw-boss hollering and snapping. In such a reductive environment very little dignity is accorded. To build relations, the manager needs to honor, encourage, and reinforce the individual's stature and personal dignity.

Probably the capstone of a good relations climate is the use of talents and interests. When men can contribute, when a manager is using their talents and curiosities, their sense of importance is enhanced. People have an array of talents; try to use as many of these talents as possible. Find out what talents they have and capitalize on them; challenge your people to use them. Broaden the employee; don't make him a specialist in narrow, routine tasks. Simply stated, people need to be well *utilized*, not just well *treated*.

USE THE ORGANIZATION FOR RESULTS

Managers are evaluated by their executives on many criteria. One prime criterion is whether his department is organized for results.

Is the department set up for effectiveness? Conversely, is the department ineffective, rigid, and limited in its output quality and quantity?

Another criterion is the ability of the department to contribute to the enterprise. Is the department launching something that other departments can use, or is it existing only for itself? A manager has responsibility to higher management, to peer management, and to employees to make his department visible. How effective is your department's public relations within your company?

Some managers stimulate output and their services enter the system, but few may know the extent, the magnitude, the quality, or the soundness of that department's contribution. The effective manager makes the services of his department and people visible. He makes known those additional capabilities of his organization that are not being used. Compare him with the manager who complains about the strain he is under and a shortage of help. Such a manager gives the impression that his organization cannot contribute more than what it is contributing and that his people are using their maximum capabilities. This image will keep work away from the organization; at the same time it does not lend itself to the manager's own career mobility or to the self-esteem of his subordinates.

Many departments are set in a permanent, rigid framework in which employees are given assignments that never vary. Too often companies force people into job descriptions rather than design jobs to fit the abilities of the employees. Many managers assume that employees are limited in their talents and thus should be pigeonholed into a limiting position. But most people would be better utilized if they were seen as being capable of filling multiple assignments. When new personnel are selected, the manager should not hire an individual to contribute only in one area. An employee should be viewed as an interchangeable contributor, able to fit into many different task forces. Job enrichment, not just job rotation, is the key.

Task-Project Managing

The very essence of the industrial world is the constant change of priorities and the content and context of assignments. As priorities change, a manager needs the critical ability to shift his personnel to those projects with the highest need. This requires flexible people as well as people with multiple capabilities. Peter Drucker takes the position that a manager wins by assigning his personnel to opportunities, not just to problems. Priorities and needs change, and as the probabilities of success change, people in management must be able to move their personnel. Job enrichment means multiple use of interests and talents.

Service,
the Essence of Effectiveness

To obtain organization balance and flexibility, be willing to rearrange employees' assignments to meet the requirements of other groups. Many managers assign their people to the services they like, focusing on their own personality needs and aspirations instead of finding out what the receiving organizations need. Stay service conscious; no matter whether you are line or staff, no matter what your functional area, your mission is to service other organizations.

This is why we stress the need for flexible employees. Every time a manager hires an applicant who claims only one capability, that manager is crippling himself and the overall organizational flexibility. The art of managing these multifunctional employees is to use them to meet as many objectives as possible, without sacrificing performance excellence. This is the genius of managing.

This built-in, multiuse capability represents the ability to revitalize or recharge an organization. The workers in a calcified group that has not been revitalized become apathetic. Job and self-destruction result.

Task force management usually results in psychological payoff for employees. Most important, it provides job variability. One of the complaints we hear over and over in employee counseling is about boring, routine, standardized jobs.

Stimulate your employees, whenever possible, with a variety of assignments; observe people under different conditions and assignments. This way you will find out where they can produce; don't box them into one assignment when they might be more effective on other assignments as well. Find out how many other things your employees can do. When a person is allowed to prove himself in different areas, he will feel he is not hamstrung; the variety will be a challenge to him. Job variety through job enrichment also encourages emotional health. With an array of assignments, a manager builds flexibility within his employees and the organization.

Another benefit of the task force approach to assignments is a decrease in overspecialization. Most companies are looking for flexibility in a manager—one who can take on multiple missions. Many managers feel that they can manage only one area, and turn down promotions in another area because they have become too much of a specialist. This may have resulted from the way they were managed. By making them specialists, the company now has rigid management.

A project task force approach provides the chance to capitalize upon the strengths of others. To know your employees and their capabilities, you must allow them to perform in different situations. Subsequently, when you get a priority assignment that calls for certain skills, you will know where the skill is and you can best bring your human powerhouses together to work on this project. When this assignment is over, the group can be disbanded and a different group with a different set of strengths can be focused on the next assignment. Your overall payoff will be an increase in the effectiveness and flexibility of the department through temporary and adaptive systems.

Some managers, because of their own compulsiveness and rigid adherence to detail, break down an assignment into numerous small parts. Assignment analysis is a meaningful approach, but to allocate small pieces of a project to different people will have little developmental value to the individuals. Allocate major shares of work. For most people a substantial share of a work assignment has higher payoff than a little bit of the assignment. An employee will quickly be bored by a meaningless tidbit, and he may become a restless and a potentially job-dissatisfied individual who will not enhance the overall group morale.

Everybody's Job Is Nobody's Job

One overall objective of a manager is to decrease role ambiguity and role conflict. Role conflict is interpersonal warfare that exists between men in organizational life through rivalry over assignments, opportunities, and functions. Let's take a look at some of the causes, which stem from what a manager is *not* doing.

The first cause for conflict of roles is overlapping assignments—giving the same assignment to two subordinates—possibly because the manager's control system is poor. Often the assignment is not clearly defined in the first place. As the two employees work toward solving the problem, they begin to come into conflict. They quickly find out they are both working on the same assignment, yet each one feels it is his assignment. This possessiveness may result in friction. Such inept management results in hostility, friction, and a breakdown in group unity.

Role conflicts occur when one man is requested to duplicate the effort of another. When an employee discovers that another person has been asked to duplicate the same effort he thought was near completion, it is like telling him that his effort isn't good enough, or that his work can't be trusted. This may result in hostility between the subordinates and between the subordinates and the manager. Neither subordinate is happy because both are placed in a compromised spot. If the work needs to be duplicated or cross-checked, the task should be given back to the same man who did the task.

A third cause of role conflict is the manager's failure to designate a leader when assigning work to a task force; thus task force members do not know who is to be held accountable. Without a leader the question of responsibility will cause role conflict. Jockeying starts among employees for the leadership role, especially if it looks to be a successful project for which the leader will be accorded more visibility. In the contest for the leader role, both physical and psychological energies are wrongly wasted on the conflict rather than on the accomplishment of the task.

MANAGEMENT AND EMPLOYEE DEVELOPMENT

One of the manager's prime responsibilities is the development of human capabilities. At times, managers function in a kind of teacher-student relationship, in which the teacher appraises and gives a "grade" to each employee for his achievements. However, management is teaching the subordinate as well as grading him. The management that emphasizes grading and discipline without thought to the growth and development of its personnel may be a decaying management.

Management development is a systematic process of planned managerial learning that stimulates the individual to improve his present performance and guides him in preparation for higher responsibilities.

Management development enables present managers to insure that tomorrow's managers will not lose the capabilities that the present management has built. In other words, management acts to insure that tomorrow's managers will not mismanage the organization's resources when important decisions are in their hands.

Dollars and Development

Management development is not done for welfare reasons or to be "nice"; rather, there is a dollars-and-cents reason. Management development maintains present organization strength and stresses the need for continued strength. Management development focuses not only on the individual, but also on organization development, assisting organizations to be more effective and preparing people to maintain the vitality of the incumbent management.

Management development plans continuity. The contingencies of disability, either mental or physical, may cause a break in management continuity. All of a sudden nobody knows who should make which decisions, and employees feel lost, wondering if the new manager will have the same philosophy and policies as the previous one. Anxiety is felt in a corporation when a key man dies, leaves, or is disabled; management development assists in meeting these contingencies and tensions.

Whenever a replacement who knows what to do can step in, the "down time" is minimal; anxiety is less compared to when a person inherits a position through a crisis decision. Management development is fair to the company, it is fair to the manager, and it is fair to employees.

To guide the career growth of its potential key personnel, a company uses management development. First of all, management development prevents managers from becoming indispensable. As long as a manager remains the only one who can manage a certain department, there is a probability that he is going to stay there. The more indispensable a manager is to his boss, the more his vertical career mobility may be in danger. Backups are important for a managerial career. One rule of thumb is two replacements for every key person to give everyone, especially the immediate organization, flexibility. A lack of managerial backups is often a sign of the early death of the organization.

Management development should be implemented for the career growth of the replacements. Many ambitious men are anxious about their progress. To retain good managers and talented individuals, attention needs to be given to their careers—another dollar-and-cents reason for management development.

Management development is best accomplished by providing employees with challenges. The word "challenge" holds meaning for development. No one grows unless he is challenged; no one grows when he has no obstacles to overcome. First, identify the shortcomings and the strengths of the individual; then plan how the training can provide challenging managerial learning experiences inside and outside the position.

On-the-Job Training

Management development occurs primarily through on-the-job experiences. In the long run, formal lectures add little toward changing behavior. The key to management development is the manager's desire to change managerial behavior through insight and "hands on" experience. The goal is better management, performance, and decision making.

Management development calls for diversified experiences. Similar experiences make superspecialists out of specialists. We are not talking about technical development. Rather we are focusing on how a person learns to manage and how he becomes a stronger manager. No one can learn how to manage unless he is allowed to manage. The opportunities to manage, to make mistakes, and to learn from those mistakes must be provided. The environment should offer diversified managerial experience and risk opportunities, and the new manager will grow as a result of learning by doing and by taking planned risks.

Challenge employees to acquire new knowledge; give them assignments where they have to acquire new information. Provide the developing candidate with the opportunity to acquire new skills, and let him practice these management skills; a cardinal philosophy of management development is the *practice of skills.*

Another principle of management development is to encourage and support risk taking, to give responsibility, and to have visible accountability. If an employee is not held accountable for results, he does not grow; if a man is not asked to take a risk and propose new action, he does not grow. Responsibility for results, rather than passive onlooking, will help employees grow. In the pursuit of management development, you must arrange conditions and provide events and assignments that release talent potential through guided risk.

The side effect from this attention to human careers is that employees get the feeling that somebody cares about their careers and talents. Because management development shows concern, they have a feeling of importance through committed involvement, and they will grow.

Make people think for themselves. Encourage them to think through their decisions and the alternatives and to be systematic in presenting their ideas. By providing alternatives for them and providing unilateral decisions as well, you are not developing them; you are making them management pygmies. This doesn't mean that you let the baby run out into the street to get hit by a car. As a manager you have a responsibility to watch over your employees. If inexperienced personnel make decisions that are way off base and are thus jeopardizing relationships and organization effectiveness, this is the time for coaching and guidance. But don't put the damper on the decision process before the person is willing to communicate what he would decide.

Goals for Growth

Employees should be asked to set goals beyond their present level of performance. When managers ask employees to accomplish tasks already accomplished—asking them to make contributions that do not increase their learning in new areas—little growth can take place. Of course, the goals must be realistic. If a manager can see that a goal can be accomplished within the environment, and he sees that the employee will profit by the growth experience, he should encourage the individual to do it. Employees should be competing against themselves to reach new goals (past performance versus new performance). This is the inner-person competition of management development.

Learning goals should be mutually established in the boss–subordinate relationship. It is fine for an employee to want to do things for his own development, but the manager should not permit an employee to do certain things at certain times. While it might be a development experience for him, the activity must first contribute to organization effectiveness. However, if the development experience fits into the composite priorities of needs, the manager and subordinate should mutually agree upon the assignments and challenges that can be given. Assignments that need accomplishing can be given differentially to those people who need to grow in different areas.

Top management, responsible for a company's management development, has to be emotionally and intellectually committed to the reality that management development is an extended learning process. It doesn't happen overnight. It is an ongoing, evolving process that is more than just exposure to a prearranged set of training courses. Also it is not built on constant home runs and perfect performance. Management development is built on errors as well as on successes. A healthy corporate climate is needed for management development to succeed—a climate that will let men and women take reasonable risks. A good coaching manager who will stand by his evolving employees as they take these decision risks is also needed.

One valuable management development technique is to have high-potential employees communicate with other management personnel. This means job rotation and exposure to higher-level meetings. It will assist the individual to go to another functional area and present a proposal. By performing different functions and communicating with different levels, he will learn the values and viewpoints of higher management. Supervisors often have biased images of employees in other departments and at other management levels. The growing foreman has no way of knowing these other men unless he is sent there to find out.

Company growth and managment effectiveness increase through improved managers. Manpower is a resource that is able to appreciate in value; it can also depreciate in value just like any other resource, and therein lies the responsibility for management development. Your organization must not allow its human assets to depreciate because it does not have the time to invest in constantly replanting the management team.

PART THREE

THE MANAGER AS MULTIPLIER

A leader is best
When people barely know he exists,
Not so good when people obey and acclaim him,
Worst when they despise him.
Fail to honor people
They fail to honor you;
But of a good leader, who talks little,
When his work is done, his aim fulfilled,
They will all say, "We did this ourselves."
—*Lao-tzu*

8

The Manager as
Change Agent

Each of us has a need to increase our influence over others.
The promotable manager who moves ahead and stays ahead on a fast
career track must have the ability to get others to see things his way
and to motivate them to take action along results-oriented lines. Managerial effectiveness in this area means influence—influence to affect existing
attitudes, to get others to give up one way of acting and rechannel
their behavior or decision making along different lines. When was the
last time you tried to influence your employees to do something different
or tried to persuade your executive to start doing something? When
was the last time you were successful in talking a fellow manager into
modifying a plan of action? When was the last time you failed to promote
a new program?

The most important elements to consider are attitudes. Rigid attitudes
to which others cling can act as a bottleneck, resisting your direction,
or as a pump, facilitating your managing. Executives who want to
implement changes necessary for the growth and vitality of their organization are becoming increasingly aware of the necessity for careful
planning and organization development. Within any organization there
are conflicting pressures for both stability and change. Those who resist
change and want to keep things the way they are attach a lot of emotional
and political weight to the fact that the current situation represents

a great investment in time, effort, and money. They often feel over-whelmed by change and see in it only the prospect of more work. If they are politically vigilant, they might perceive the change as disrupting to their relationships, diminishing their power, or adversely affecting their own department's visibility and exposure. They want to conserve the certainties with which they are familiar. These are the status quo maintainers.

Zest and commitment for change spring from a striving for improvement by those in the organization who are dissatisfied with the present situation and who want different achievements or a greater sense of task and personal payoff. Change often stems from these managers' frustration when what is being done falls short of what could be done. Those managers who act as change agents recognize that corporations cannot meet the future just by doing more of what they have been doing.

As he matures, a manager should gain experience and, hopefully, wisdom. But he sometimes gains ossification instead. He may simply be stagnating, doing the same old things in the same old way. One of management's most basic skills is to be an agent of change. The accomplishment of tasks through the commitment of others is the key to effective managing. The word "manage" implies influence; management's job is to influence people to start and to complete activities leading toward a goal, and to coordinate effectively the commitments of different people.

INFLUENCING ATTITUDES

We all need and depend on other people. The pressurized atmosphere of the organization world shows us that we don't totally control our own lives. All of us are bound by interlocked commitments—or lack of them—with others. Often, to accomplish tasks in our own department, we need to get work done in somebody else's department. Here we may run into blocks, stalemates, and resistance. Probably a definitive mark of the successful manager is his ability to extract work from other areas, thus enabling his own organization to proceed. The ability to influence the attitude of others, to overcome resistance whenever it is encountered, distinguishes the achieving manager from the one who exists as a reactive model of organization stagnation.

What are attitudes? An attitude is basically the way in which a person perceives himself, other people, and events, and the way he emotionally relates to his work. People behave as they do because of how they see things, not necessarily because of what is true or real. Verbal appeals to logic by a manager do not necessarily influence employees, because people are not always logical. Since job commitment is emotionally, not logically, based, it is of the utmost importance that the manager be sensitive to his people's perceptions—how they see the organization world about them, how they see themselves, how they see task situations, and how they see him as a manager.

Some attitudes serve as standards of judgment: they determine things a person will consider to be worthwhile or of high priority. These standards of judgment differ greatly. Project requests and departmental events that are important to George may be valueless to Sam.

Because attitudes are basic predispositions that determine the way an individual will experience a situation, they greatly influence the filtering process we perform on the requests that are aimed at us. For example, one man may see an inquiry about the status of his project simply as a request for information. Another, perhaps because of an attitude of dislike or fear, might assume that the request is an attempt to spy.

No two people hear or see the same thing. All of us interpret the interpersonal world around us; all of us bias the signals we receive. We tend to hear and see what we want to hear and see. Managers who try to deal with "reality" rather than facing the fact of people's selective perception have not yet grasped the psychological fact that, where behavior is concerned, the way the world is perceived is more important then the way it is. One of management's responsibilities is to single out employees' distinctly personal views of events, situations, and other people.

Attitudes also have impact in the area of motivation. Negative attitudes can prevent movement toward desired objectives or, in some cases, can cause movement in a direction opposite to what is desired. Negative attitudes often result when an employee is focusing on a perceived danger rather than on the purpose of the task at hand. Psychologically, he may be more concerned with how the task affects his self-interest than with the objectives and how they can best be achieved. He devotes too much emotional energy to examining what can go wrong or how he can be hurt, instead of committing his energy to achieving the goal. Negative reactions happen when a situation is disturbing, threatening, or painful to our self-concept or self-esteem.

On the other hand, we tend to react in a favorable way and with a positive attitude toward those things which agree with our self-concept and thus pose no threat to us. This positive feeling helps us to achieve our objectives, support others, cooperate, and produce.

Attitudes assist us to arrange behavior options into a hierarchical order of preference. Consider a manager with a personnel surplus who has to let a staff member go. One man in his department has four children, his wife is in the hospital, and he is doing an average job. Another employee—single, 25 years old—is a crackerjack performer, at the top of the manager's merit chart. But because this manager has a particular set of attitudes he lets the young, unmarried engineer go—his best man.

Another manager, with another set of attitudes, in the same situation, might decide to let the engineer with the four children go. The problem is the same, the situation is the same, but the attitudes are different and result in different management decisions.

Why Resistance to Change?

One challenge confronting a manager is how best to introduce necessary changes. People resist change because they are generally content to do the familiar, they are emotionally secure in knowing the ropes, they feel confident, and they have mastered a situation. People want to be masters of their own fate. A suggestion of change conjures up the unknown and all its attendant fears. When people are asked to change, their psychological security is threatened, with the result that they may directly or indirectly resist the change.

Proposals for change may also cause employees to fear that they are going to lose something: their income may be adversely affected, their position may become insecure, their power may be diminished. A request for change may appear to the employee or fellow manager to threaten his self-interest or some highly valued beliefs. Changes, even if objectively favorable to the individual, are often seen subjectively as being less valuable. Both "Danger!" and "Sounds like a good deal" are in the eye of the beholder.

Suggestions for change are often seen as criticisms of competence. In reality, most business decisions that require change have little personal orientation. They are task-centered, problem-oriented, situationally determined. Nevertheless, when asked to change, many feel that their competence is being challenged, and the results may be resistance, moodiness, and anxiety.

Frequently, employees resist change because they do not want to see themselves simply as cogs in a machine. Pride is an important ingredient of the healthy human personality. No one wants to feel victimized by another's whims. When a manager calls for change, the individual may feel he is just an object being arbitrarily programmed. A supervisor can generate and intensify resistance if he makes people feel they are serflike beings who are forced to comply in a feudal managerial climate. Being somebody else's peon is not conducive to motivation, especially when it results from insensitive management behavior. When people are forced to change, with no control or say about the changes that will affect them, they are likely to lose their sense of importance.

Resistance to change can be amplified and stimulated by group pressures. If a group member of a task project team feels that the others in the group may be opposed to a given course of proposed action, he will be hesitant to go along by favoring it. He may be wondering what sort of interpersonal rejection he will suffer if he lines up his thinking with that of his boss. Group folkways do operate, and the effective manager must be sensitive to the social impact of the changes he institutes.

Many times people resist change when they are too personally involved in the existing method. They may have worked for months creating whatever system is currently in effect. Thus constructive changes are seen as destructive to the individual's own personal efforts. The manager who succeeds in making changes does not bulldoze through another's objections, but takes them into account in his plan to overcome this resistance.

Resistance is not caused solely by obstinate human nature. Employees resist change when they are mishandled by a management that is not considerate, sensitive, predictive, or organized enough to plan for the introduction and dialogue needed. Understandably, people resist change when they mistrust those who are proposing it, when the reasons for the change are ambiguous and undefined, or when they are not involved in its planning. They resist when the social relationships and mores of the work group are ignored, when they fear inadequacy or failure, or when they are satisfied with the status quo. People also resist when they anticipate an inadequate reward for making the change, whether that reward be financial or nonfinancial. And they resist when there is lack of information about the changes, causing fear and rumors. Change must be carefully planned.

OVERCOMING RESISTANCE: SEDUCTION OR HONESTY

Logical arguments are not, by themselves, effective instruments for overcoming resistance. Much as we may like to think of ourselves as rational beings, usually our emotions are the major determinant of what we do or resist doing. To convert resistance to willing cooperation, consider the emotional component of employee attitudes. Attitude change cannot be forced. Managers can force people to work, but they can't force them to change their attitudes. A manager who uses his formal rank to win the inning may well lose the ball game of overall leader effectiveness. The department must be ready for change and employees must be willing for change if their redirected behavior is to lead to task-associated cooperation and sustained performance. It is essential to remember that at times of change, facts are less important than feelings. Invest your time in understanding how your staff perceives the new way, and listen to their doubts and fears.

The group leader. The first step in overcoming resistance is to look for the informal group leader. He is the individual who is crucial to the implementation of your plans, because the group looks to him for approval, advice, and protection. Often employees do not go to their supervisor for open discussions, but instead go to this group-recognized leader. Take him into your confidence and deal with him individually. Find out his feelings, his reactions, and what he thinks will be necessary to get the group to understand and accept the change. Get him on your bandwagon first and then let him help you influence the group.

Communication. Communicate the reasons for the change, and address yourself especially to the false notions that build up about an anticipated change. Let people know that the change is not personal but task-centered. Eliminate any perceived threat to individual vested interests. The mature manager lets his people know that he respects their competence.

Group participation. Enlist the group's participation and ask for their opinions and suggestions before implementing the change. Involving people early can be important if you respect and utilize the group's opinions. When asking for suggestions and opinions, you alert those involved to the changes; you do not spring the change on them. If you are sincere about stimulating change suggestions, the people involved should be alerted to the need, and feel that they are contributing their ideas. Then they will have a sense of belonging, of importance, and of sharing in the future success.

This sense of being needed is one of the most important elements in the development of attitudes conducive to your plans. Ask your staff for other ways in which problems could be solved or the new objectives achieved. This style of handling change not only satisfies the need for participation, but it has the added advantage of possibly generating better alternatives than those originally considered. We heard of one instance in which a corporate management, after spending over $100,000 on an inadequate technical system, in desperation asked employees what could be done. Suggestions came that not only solved the problem, but showed how some of the misspent money could be recovered.

Honesty. Openly discuss the advantages as well as the pitfalls involved in the change. When discussing the negative aspects, let your staff know that your eyes are open and that you appreciate the problems they will be facing. In a sense, the leader beats his people to the punch by pointing out the possible negative aspects of the change.

Of course, you must also stress and highlight the positive side. Emphasize achievement opportunities, job variety and diversification, and credit for accomplishment.

The employees' point of view. Try to explain the change in the context of your subordinates' goals and values. What is in it for them? Your success at persuasion depends ultimately upon your ability to discuss the subject in terms of the self-interests of those being persuaded. Selfish interests and self-protecting perceptions should be acknowledged, not denied, in the change process. If such interests are not addressed, the employee will not have his "real" questions answered. He will not be interested in doing something that he considers is only for the benefit of the group or the boss. He will be constructively motivated only if he sees some benefit for himself in the change. The wise manager will analyze situations from his employees' point of view and emphasize those aspects that promise rewards to the individual.

Another approach is to make the person indirectly realize that he is not attacking the job in a way his supervisor would like. This should be conveyed without inviting antagonism. One way of doing this is to draw attention to what others are doing and to express interest in their approaches. For example: "I just came back from Beta Electronics, and this is how they are doing it there," or, "At the annual meeting of the Congress of Heuristic Associations for National Gear Engineers, they talked about experimenting with this approach, Jim. . . ." In this manner, the supervisor indicates interest in, and tacit approval of, the new method, while giving the employee a sense of participation in the making of the decision.

DON'T BOTHER ME NOW

The proper timing can do much to help implement change. When a change is to be made, be prompt in its announcement. The manager's worse enemy is rumor. Rumors start because management waits too long to give out crucial information concerning changes that will affect the individual's work life. Avoid the blunt announcement. Discuss the problems first and explain the reasons why change is needed.

The proper timing can also insure employee emotional security. By allowing them time to learn new methods, along with providing training programs, you communicate to them that you appreciate their need for time to relearn and to adjust. People fear least those things they know they will have time to absorb and learn. By approaching the fearful change gradually, and picking up knowledge or techniques that will help them face what is at the end of the road, employees will be better able to deal with the challenge of change.

When explaining the change, confront, don't avoid, their questions. Explain why the change is important to the company and to them. Discuss all the ramifications. If change is going to affect individuals' jobs, or if they have to learn new jobs, let them know they have been selected to make the change because of their abilities, not because of their shortcomings. Openly level with them and explore how the change will affect their lives. They will be better able to cope with change and with the threat it engenders when they fully understand and have available as much information as possible.

If the change is a major one, extending over time, it is best to institute it in progressive stages, which are more palatable and easier to absorb. Be sure your employees know the total picture of changes and when those changes will stop. Avoid having changes follow too rapidly after one another. Space them out and give your employees time to assimilate and digest them.

If the change is an unpopular one, determine if it is possible to sweeten it with a popular trade-off. For example, in a manufacturing area the production workers on the assembly line were upset when completely new equipment was installed which required them to learn new procedures. To offset their anxiety, management announced that the workers would be allowed to do different jobs up and down the line rather than being in one spot as they had been in the past. With a popular trade-off, it is possible to lessen the threat involved in a change that is seen negatively.

If possible, don't let a change build the status of one member of the staff at the expense of other employees. Determine in advance whether the change will disturb the group's social relationships and avoid making changes that might cause interpersonal jealousy and disruption. Remember that chickens have been known to peck to death other chickens who disturb the farmyard pecking order.

Show the group your interdependence and your need for them. Communicate that you are seeking the help of the individuals and the group. It requires managerial maturity to be able to say to another that you need him. This provides the group members with a sense of importance, a feeling of identification with the boss, and an indication that their efforts are recognized.

A leader can also provide a challenge for his people by turning a problem into a competition. However, he must challenge them through respect for their talents and abilities, not by degrading or demeaning their skills. Present a job and its attendant problems by showing your people where the challenge lies and how some national experts handle the implementation.

Attitudes are the emotional lenses through which everyone perceives his job life. Attitudes determine our reactions to people and to organization situations. When executives seek to direct employee activity so as to promote results-oriented commitments and cooperative enterprise, they are well advised to apply their sensitivity to the point of origin of human activity—the emotional basis of attitudes. An astute manager will find ways to meet the different forces that operate in each of his subordinates. For one subordinate, the appeal might be ego satisfaction; for another, the need to belong and to be accepted; for still another, the desire for security and comfort, or pride.

Through such sensitivity, the manager can provide his staff with corrective emotional lenses to help modify their attitudes and change their performance and decision making. Properly altered attitudes will evoke reactions in line with the framework the manager seeks to establish. Appropriate attitudes are the starting point for business activity, for energetic, willing activity in support of a manager's program. The door must be open to harmonious and noteworthy achievement, and the best technique is to influence attitudes, the key to managerial effectiveness.

9

Why Staff People Fail

The traditional dichotomy that has existed between line and staff positions is beginning to fade. Historically, line people were thought to be the prime movers and gadflys of the organization, functioning in the core areas of the company's business. Staff people were assistants whose sole duty was to serve line management. Such organization images and relationship barriers don't get us very far today. Staff people are making a lot of decisions that influence line activities, and much line activity has the purpose of supporting staff management's requirements. There are staff people with regulating authority and people in line operations who function as staff.

So, instead of dividing an organization into competitive wings and factions, it would be more productive to focus on the common interests and purposes that characterize the successful and achieving corporation.

Although the concept of line people and staff people has structural value, it is a stereotyped bias to think of them as separate, distinct categories. The manager must not be too rigid to see the realities of organization dynamics. It is more useful to perceive that many people function in both line and staff roles at different times to meet the different needs of the organization. In the microsociety we call the corporation, traditional organization distinctions often blur.

This chapter focuses on the staff role that all of us, in or out of management, fulfill at various times. The function of staff is to influence line management's attitudes to implement change. When staff people function as change agents in an organization, they must do so by persuasiveness, competence, and personal contribution. Staff people often have the job of making an impact or getting others to voluntarily support their ideas. Staff effectiveness is at once one of the most challenging and one of the most frustrating roles.

One problem of organization life is that many people do not have the insight into interpersonal relationships that will allow them to sell their ideas, contribute meaningfully to changing the organization, and move toward achieving organization goals. The inevitable frustration that results when they are unable to move in these positive directions takes its toll in wasted talent, anti-organizational activity, and corporate and personal stagnation. How many good ideas and significant contributions die before seeing the light of day because their originator could not deal adequately with interpersonal relationships.

Management mutters foul oaths about the rebels and young turks who don't know their place; young staff men complain about the old neanderthals who are out of touch with modern concepts and organization opportunities. Whose fault is it? Both. Management that reacts defensively whenever a new idea is mentioned is a liability that few corporations and their shareholders can afford. Like the boss who told his subordinates (and he meant *subordinates*), "I don't want you to be yes-men. When I say no, I want you to say no." Or the boss who said, "When I want your opinion, I'll give it to you."

But what about the other half of the interaction, the staff person who is unable to play effectively by the rules of the system? Some staff people learn the ropes early, some learn later, and some never learn. An examination of the poles of the success–failure dimension may throw some light on how to function effectively in a staff role.

ARE THEY WITH YOU?

Considerable staff failure occurs when a staff person does not get initial agreement that there is a problem or that improvements in an existing system can be effected. The ineffective individual tends to begin with solutions rather than with problem definition and problem concurrence through mutual explorations. He starts off with the last step instead of beginning at the beginning. He walks in, sits down, and starts talking problem solving; but his caught-cold management customer is thinking, "What problem?"

The successful individual realizes that he must start out by demonstrating that a need exists. He knows how to highlight and explain the problem through mutual communication, not by singing solo. Many staff people are so preoccupied with selling their change that they forget to lay the groundwork. Although line management might have done the requisite thinking and gone through all the data and studies, many times they have not.

When you are introducing change, don't talk about the proposed change; talk about the need for the change. Give your audience the benefit of systematic questioning. Once you gain initial agreement about the problem and convince everyone that a change would be beneficial, you have succeeded in the crucial step of making sure that everybody is operating in the same ball park. You will fail in your staff capacity if you talk about going to bat and hitting home runs but forget to ask management if they even want to play.

DON'T BE AN EXPERT

Often resistance to change has little or nothing to do with the technical or methodological aspects of the change. Nor is the resistance directed at the idea itself. Rather it is directed at the staff man and the way he has presented himself in the politico-personal world in which he operates. Perhaps he has acted like a self-conceived and self-portrayed expert who has all the answers, in which case he will undoubtedly get negative reactions. Everyone has to protect and project a self-image, but some people are more abrasive than others, and they tend to come on strong through their mannerisms, their words, their physical bearing and stance, and the intonations in their voice. The psychological message transmitted by such a person is that of a human projectile who sees himself as a combination savior and sage. He will be resisted and rebuffed; and his ideas will fail because of himself.

The staff person who succeeds, and who helps his boss succeed, plays the roles of counselor and mutually exploring catalyst. He has learned that management does need his counsel but does not need a bulldozer-style indoctrination. To be effective you must learn how to blend your customer's ideas with your own. Don't be a lecturer on how to do it right. Ask yourself what useful knowledge others have that will make your mutual ideas work. Assume neither a superior nor subservient posture, but a parallel and consultative role.

TUNE IN TO MANAGEMENT

The ineffective individual in a staff position is often unwilling to listen with an open mind when line management tries to point out the blind spots in his proposal—those political problems or operating situations he might have failed to consider. For the most part, line managers will be cooperative and helpful. They have been over the course themselves and are willing to give pointers to anyone on the way up. They realize that life in the organization world is competitive but that it functions through interactive understandings. When they see a young, zestful, vigorous staff man come in with new ideas, they will probably try to point out to him his situational naïveté. Generally speaking, they are doing it to be helpful. But at this juncture an ineffective staff employee will get defensive and tense up his "proposal" muscles. He does not tune in to the problems that have been pointed out, and he becomes so preoccupied with winning, with the beauty of his own idea, and with the intricacy of his system, that he gets caught in an ego trap. This self-preoccupation and engrossment in his own technology and sales pitch will make him oblivious to messages conveyed by the line manager, who may feel his status, accomplishments, or political relationships are being threatened. If you don't listen to the practical considerations which the customer tries to inform you about, and which perhaps you did not think of or evaluate before making your presentation, your proposal is doomed. Our suggestion is to listen, to be adaptable, and to be receptive to realities other people point out. Let management cooperate with you in the creation of a mutual program.

"I DON'T GET NO RESPECT"

Not infrequently, management says its reason for not buying a staff proposal is that there is something wrong or deficient in the idea itself. Certainly this may be the case, but often that is not the real reason. Often the issue is the manager's concern over whether the staff person really respects his opinions and needs. Staff people are useless if they cannot engender committed implementation of their ideas by line management. Many staff people forget that they are the guest, not the host. They forget that line management is the customer, and that his feelings and perceptions are worth listening to. Not only that, but line management's emotional commitment is vital to the success of the idea; you are most likely to obtain this commitment if you let him participate. He may be misinformed about some subjects he discusses, but a lot of his contributions will be sound.

All of us need to question whether we are respecting the opinions of our audience members, whether we genuinely care about them. You must treat your customers as individuals whose opinions you respect. If you simply go through the mechanical motions of listening, you won't convince anyone. Such listeners sit in the executive's office and give him their token attention, nodding their heads occasionally, but they really couldn't care less about what the man has to say. Before presenting any idea, you should be sure you are genuinely open to other people's ideas. *Staff effectiveness starts with one's attitudes.*

Ask yourself whether you feel the people you are serving deserve respect. If your answer is no, you are probably listening to them as part of a manipulative, tactical plan. Many staff people in organizations are playing a part. For them, letting management participate is nothing more than tactics; they want to fool management into believing they are interested in them and their ideas.

If this is your attitude, then you have missed the point. Don't play "let's pretend" in this area. People can and do detect phony, put-on behavior. Genuine concern for the other person is called for. When another feels that you really desire his participation, he will also know that you care about him as an individual and that you see worth in his ideas. In this atmosphere a fulfilling give-and-take relationship can exist, and much progress can be made. Have a listening ear and a seeing eye.

The staff person who perceives this discussion as too "soft," as having too many human relations elements, is making a tragic mistake. The staff person who believes he and his technique are infallible is also heading for trouble. There is much evidence that people respond in a manner similar to the way in which they are treated. It is unfortunate that many staff employees will choose to fight with the line manager rather than cooperate with him. The result is a win–lose game with little progress in sight for anyone.

REAL REASONS FOR RESISTANCE

Another pitfall for the staff employee is the resistance he will face due to the sociopolitical change that is inherent in any proposal. The technical side of the idea may be fine, but as the line manager listens, he is listening for the relationship impacts that will occur if the staff person's suggestion is implemented.

There is an official organization that is represented by organization charts with people nicely arranged in spaced boxes. There is also the informal world with its unofficial social relationships that are established so that managers can be effective. It is this nonstructured world that is the real organization, that gets the work through the system, that achieves the objectives. So when the staff employee talks about his technological change, his new procedure, or his new method, the executives on the receiving end are not listening to that alone. They are listening to how it will affect their power platform; they are listening for possible social and political changes.

The staff man may be unintentionally naïve; in fact, his naïveté may come through more than the quality of his idea. He does not live day in and day out in the operational world; he does not have intimate contact with all the interpersonal subtleties that exist in management. He can't possibly be that close to all the power trade-offs and informal agreements that are made between managers who work together; he is the outsider.

Thus the need for you, as a staff man, to remain open becomes critical. You must listen for clues and signals that will guide you in how to mold your proposal to fit into the very human world in which your customer operates and is presently making things happen.

COMMUNICATE WITH THEM, NOT AT THEM

Another characteristic of the ineffective staff man is that he is an overwhelming communicator. This is not to say he can't speak well; rather, he speaks too well. His profuse expostulation and peripatetic meanderings through the lexicon are fabulously splendiferous.

Our suggestion here is to cease the razzle-dazzle and verbal footwork. Speak plainly, simply, and directly to the point; do not try to impress with the vastness of your knowledge or with complicated figures. To overcommunicate insults others' intelligence, and their translation of what you have said may not be what you intended: "I know you believe you understand what you think I said but I'm not sure you realize that what you heard is not what I meant."

The customer should obtain a clear, simple picture of your proposal and recommendations. You can promote his ability to do so if you put the proposal in terms of his experience. Try to discover what experiences the line people had or are having now that relate to your proposal. Speak their language; refer to things that they understand. People agree with you when they understand what you're saying, not when they feel overwhelmed with obscure verbiage. If an idea is accepted because it was ramrodded through rather than understood, in the future they will probably be dissatisfied with you and your ideas.

Two other communication principles suggest themselves in this connection: (1) speak the truth, and (2) present yourself so that people can believe that you are speaking the truth. Although speaking the truth is essential, it is not sufficient. Document, be specific, and quantify, when you can. Avoid the unsupported superlatives that automatically conjure up disbelief. Speak with taste and with grace.

NO SHOVING

An effective staff employee has patience. He shows a willingness to install a program at others' convenience. Be wise enough to know that it takes time to put any change successfully into operation. We are reminded of the following poem:

The Dachshund

There was a dachshund once so long,
    He hadn't any notion
How long it took to notify
    His tail of his emotion.

And thus it was, that while his eyes
    Were filled with woe and sadness,
His little tail went wagging on
    Because of previous gladness.

The successful staff person realizes that there is often a time delay between an idea's acceptance and its implementation. Encourage your proposal's acceptance with a nudge, not a shove. Never let the customer feel he is being pushed or sold. Your success depends on the evolving relationship you establish, and you must not jeopardize that relationship by being pushy. Do not assume that you have power in your own right. Your power emanates from the goodness of your ideas and the cumulative, evolving relationships and reputation that you build.

Sometimes a staff manager feels it is safe to shove because he walks in the power shadow of another man. Someone who is failing in his staff role may well use the shadow he walks in to parlay influence and attempt to force his ideas through. The line manager may temporarily agree, in order to get the staff man out of his office. But the long-range probability is that this staff man is destined for organizational self-destruct.

If a red flag in the form of resistance from management does appear, do not try to bulldoze the program through. Instead, together search for ways to accommodate the manager's tender spot without materially affecting the worth of the total proposal. Rather than putting on your battle armor, be receptive to suggestions from management on how to modify the program. One skill called for here is ingenuity. You must figure out how to modify your proposal so as to get most of the proposal elements, but not the objectionable one, into effect. Another quality needed is maturity, since you must be willing to consider and accommodate the thinking of other people. Finally, personal flexibility is needed: It may be better to win a commitment to three-fourths of the proposal than to put yourself into a win-lose struggle in which you may lose everything.

Because the effective idea broker is a mediator and a bargainer, he tends to see resistance not as a threat but as a useful indicator that something is beginning to go wrong. He pauses and tries to discover what it is that is getting out of kilter. This is the time for diagnosis, not the time for increased pressure and force. Explore the difficulty, facilitate communication and understanding, and then determine what needs to be corrected. Do not turn to the hard sell. Realize that every man is justified in his own mind, and that "a man convinced against his will is of the same opinion still." Benjamin Franklin, who acted in a persuasive role many times in his career, advocated the soft sell in these words:

> The way to convince another is to state your case moderately and accurately. Then scratch your head, or shake it a little and say that is the way it seems to you, but that, of course, you may be mistaken about it. This causes your listener to receive what you have to say, and, as like as not, turn about and try to convince you of it, since you are in doubt. But if you go at him in a tone of positiveness and arrogance, you only make an opponent of him.

PUTTING IT IN WRITING

It is vital that a staff manager present his ideas in an understandable and motivating way. The following suggestions may help in making a written proposal.

1. *Simplify the written proposal* to decrease the complexity to the point where it can be understood easily. A proposal filled with technical jargon, even if it is to be read by experts, is a suspicious-looking one.

2. *Put your summary and action recommendations on page 1* of the proposal. Don't make your reader wade through the whole package to find out what you are proposing.

3. *Offer a number of alternative solutions.* Don't give just one idea on how to solve a problem: give several and their possible negative and positive consequences. You may feel one approach is clearly preferable, but by presenting several you communicate that you have given some thought to the matter and that it is not your intent to railroad through the first idea that comes along. Do give the alternatives in order of priority, however.

4. *Present the implementation.* Show how the proposal can be put into effect. It is much easier to identify and describe a problem than to spell out specifically how it should be solved. By providing a clear,

step-by-step road map of where we go from here, you greatly enhance your chances of selling the proposal.

5. *Put all the documentation and compiled data into an appendix* to the proposal. Do not clutter up the central part of the proposal with charts, graphs, and statistics. Your reader will be better able to follow your thought progression if the flow of main ideas is not interrupted.

6. *Mold your presentation* to fit the existing framework, terminology, and objectives of the reader with whom you are working. How does the proposal fit into existing conditions, procedures, and personnel peculiarities?

In summary, present your proposal in such a way that all the line manager needs to do is say yes or no to the proposed change. If the staff person has done all his work, the majority of the line manager's questions have already been anticipated and answered in the document itself. The manager can just focus on making the decision.

CONVINCING THE BOSS

Just as students psych out their college professors, it is possible for the staff manager to learn how and when to approach his boss so as to insure success. The following suggestions may help you in getting over some of the barriers between you and your executives.

1. Mutual identification and acceptance of the problem are essential. You and your executive should mutually define what the need and target are. Be sure you are offering a solution to a problem the boss is concerned about, not expending great energy on something that doesn't need to be done at all.

2. Involve your executive in developing possible solutions. He may or may not have suggestions, but if he has, it is imperative that you get them. His participation will make it partly his idea.

3. When you give your executive the completed staff work, be sure you have identified both the positive payoffs and the negative risks of your alternatives. Predict and spell out the gain-to-loss ratio. If the executive can review both the pros and cons of an idea, he will not feel he is being sold a bill of goods.

4. Although it is ethical for you to identify the negative aspects of your idea, you owe it to yourself to focus on the idea's strengths. Stress the aspects of the idea that are most compatible with the customer's needs and your primary alternative.

5. Present your idea at the proper time. All of us have mood swings: You should anticipate and be sensitive to the times when your executive

is most receptive. Explore what his emotional state is *before* you present your proposal.

6. Presell your ideas. You shouldn't be running in and out of the boss's office with every little piece of information, but that does not preclude you from alerting him to developments. On the contrary, you should be planting seeds in his mind that can germinate over time.

7. Indirectly bring out whatever payoffs for your boss that may result from your proposed change. If there are positive outcomes from him, let him know it with graciousness.

8. Your approach should stress that an opportunity is presenting itself. Do not stress the consequences of not changing; if you appeal to fear, you may block yourself in your effort to influence people. Instead, let your approach be one of *genuine concern* over the problem. Your tone should not be one of panic, but of optimism about the mutual gains that will result.

DON'T GO AWAY ANGRY

In staff work your patience will be tested often. You must deal with lots of obstacles, both technical and human, if you are to achieve your objectives. Therefore, if you want to effect your change you must develop your capacity to be persistent.

There is good reason to persist. Probably a significant amount of the activity going on around you is wasted. It could and should be eliminated (the old system is not working well). But in creating something new, you may have to tear down something old. You will find human resistance to any effort to change the status quo. Some line executives you encounter will try you to the limit, and you may want to turn away from any effort to improve things in their department. But don't let yourself do this. When you turn away, be sure it is because of an operating reality and not because your feelings were hurt. Forget about your feelings, and instead look after the interests of your organization. Make a staff decision on that basis, not in terms of your needs. Even if you do get walked on, you will be more contented with yourself and your job—and the organization will be better off—because of your perseverance.

If you are successful in the brokerage of your ideas you will reap the reward of being recognized not just as a staff man, but as an internal consultant. People will seek you out, your judgment will be trusted and valued, and your opinion highly regarded.

10

Achieving Motivation Release

Why is there such a high incidence of industrially related mental illness? Why are so many employees dissatisfied with their jobs? Why are large corporate bodies suffering a visible loss of talented people to smaller businesses? Why has the costly migration of human talent become a pattern in the careers of today's aspiring executives?

Less visible than these problems, however, is the costly incidence of on-the-job retirement. What about those unmotivated people who stay on the company payroll and stagnate through their entire corporate cradle-to-grave existence? Granted, in some cases the capability is just not there. But the sad truth is that huge reservoirs of human vitality lie untapped because people's talents are used restrictively, or not at all. A person who can't find his job a vehicle for personal fulfillment and occupational excitement often drifts into a work station mentality. His day becomes a series of coffee breaks punctuated by long lunch hours. His statements at his 25-year-gold-watch party could well be the same self-indictment of job apathy expressed by J. Alfred Prufrock, a character in one of T. S. Eliot's poems: "I have measured out my life in coffee spoons."

Putting aside for the moment the mental health repercussions of these situations, the cost factor remains, and such motivation waste is debilitating to an organization whose prime objective is innovation and the achievement of its objectives. We suggest that these expensive problems might be partially alleviated by understanding that motivation comes from within the employee. It is not generated externally. Obvious though this statement may seem, it is this salient point of view of employee motivation, and a grasp of the nuances and complexities of this concept, that would result in more satisfied, committed employees—and managers.

THE MYTHS OF MOTIVATION

Before exploring the releasing climate for motivation, let's define what motivation is not. Many managers sincerely believe that their approach is effective, and cannot understand why their employees are unresponsive to management's motivational beliefs and practiced manipulations.

The accountability myth, or "Don't throw me into that briar patch!" Consider the manager who, to save his staff embarrassment or lost time by their doing an assignment incorrectly, insists on prescribing and resolving every detail. With the best of intentions, he gives his experienced secretary and his qualified subordinates explicit directions on each assignment, and hovers over them. Every item must be examined at length; if his employees volunteer to tackle a problem unassisted, our over-the-shoulder manager says, "Don't worry, I'll take care of it."

One can question this manager's desire to spare an employee the accountability of handling a project unassisted or to try to protect him from making a wrong decision. More often than not, a manager's vision is blocked by the misconception that employees dislike responsibility, prefer detailed directions, and fear being held accountable for their work. By understanding that a core part of a person's job motivation is pride in self-initiated abilities, this manager may loosen the reins and discover that his personnel are adept at handling things in his absence, that they can control their own projects, and that they prefer to answer for their own decisions.

The paycheck myth, or "Money will buy you happiness." A second widely held belief is that employees work primarily for money. For example, a well-meaning machine shop manager is approached by a competent employee who expresses job discontent. The manager, sincerely wanting to see him satisfied in his work, thinks the situation over and offers him a raise. The employee's face brightens, but after several days he becomes increasingly moody and casual in his performance.

This example illustrates that money does not have a sustaining effect in motivating performance and that the pay envelope cannot give a man a sense of achievement or involvement in his work. There are some things money can do—if guaranteeing a man's appearance on the job and routine performance are the only objectives—but money cannot buy a man's interest. To the manager who insists that a solid paycheck every week provides all the job identification that is necessary, we would suggest a maxim from Seneca: "Fidelity bought with money is overcome by money."

The external stimulation myth, or "Carrots and sticks." Some executives treat their staff like a rambunctious group of five-year-olds. Often logic is ineffective, so the gimmicky approach is to resort to other methods of getting desired results—gold stars, second desserts, or longer recesses. Another approach is to propose some type of contest; within minutes, the most difficult group of children should be calmed with the promise of external reward and an appeal to the competitive spirit. If these steps fail, only one path remains: exercise authority, speak from a stance of power and control.

These methods are inept in dealing with adults. Yet they are exactly the tactics some managers employ to motivate their staff. Such ill-informed managers offer an outside reward—a bonus, time off, or a company pin—to the employee who most successfully attains the prearranged goal. Rather than stimulating competitions, such an approach only tends to breed mistrust, disunity, and resentment. *Performance commitment results from the employee's inner desire to work because of the intrinsic meaningfulness of the work.*

When the authoritarian approach fails, an insensitive manager may go a step further and use fear, threat, or even force. Fear of humiliation is often the superimposed impetus to execute job tasks. Implicit in this type of "herdmanship" behavior are a manager's attitudes and the communication of those attitudes to his employees of his superiority, authority, and domination needs.

Perhaps a concise assessment of this type of manager comes from the poet Robert Browning, who wrote, "The great mind [leader] knows the power of gentleness, one only tries force because persuasion fails." A manager who confuses external pressure with the self-released, internal elements that constitute motivation is severely handicapped in his managerial development and in his own performance effectiveness.

THE MOTIVATION PYRAMID

To better present these intrinsic factors, we have organized a structure known as the motivation pyramid. The pyramid form is appropriate, not only because its structure relies on a layering process, where each layer is an additional foundation for the higher layers, but also because a pyramid is complex and many-sided. It is this multiple convergence toward a pinnacle that makes a pyramid structure ideal to illustrate the components, as well as the release of motivated behavior.

Layer One

The bottom, or first layer, of the pyramid is made up of the different and unique biographical ingredients of each individual. Just as a gourmet cook is familiar with many spices and seasonings, knowing when and how to use each one, so is an effective manager aware that there are several past motivating factors within each individual, that no two people are ever "seasoned" alike, and that the handling of these life events must differ with each person. Let's consider some of these different factors.

Job expectations. Depending on one's state in life, age, past job and boss experiences, and so forth, each employee has his own monogrammed job expectations. For example, one employee, a 56-year-old grandfather, may enjoy accounting, and want to spend the day uninterrupted while tackling involved financial discrepancies in his company's accounts. When 5 o'clock comes he may not think of these problems until the next day. His hobbies, health, and family life are most important to him, and a full, steady day of desk-bound accounting problems, without "people problems," is his job expectation.

On the other hand, another employee, a 32-year-old bachelor, is ambitious, energetic, and happy to be always on the go. As new products specialist in the marketing development department of a large corporation, he is continually traveling, rushing to meetings, and dealing with a wide range of people. His job duties and the activities of his private life almost coincide: His closest friends are business associates and he is able to pursue his creative interests of public speaking and photography during his frequent business trips.

Were we to interchange these employees' jobs, the expectations and personal needs of both men would be grossly incompatible with the positions they were assuming, and their self-sustaining motivation would disappear.

The motivating manager will assess a man's interests, job expectations, and personality needs before assigning him jobs. He thereby will avoid creating a marginal job situation and climate characterized by low, self-initiating behavior and job discomfort.

Skills and abilities. Also related to preassignment expectation are technical skills and personal abilities. By recognizing an employee's talents and skills, whether this be through formal training or through his innate ability, a manager should be able to match a man's talents to his work and thereby increase the individual's contribution.

Although recognition and utilization of ability seem vital for motivation release, often a person's capability and areas of drive are not immediately discernible. For example, when interviewed for a job, an employee with a degree in economics indicated that his particular interest was market research. After six months on the job, his statistical ability and analytical competence proved more than adequate, but his supervisor made some further observations. The employee easily and quickly developed a rapport with people; various persons in the department and throughout the building came to him with job-related problems. At one point, this employee was able to avert a heated argument between two other analysts in the department.

The supervisor also noted that, although the employee professed to enjoy research work, his attention frequently strayed. The supervisor learned of a personnel opening at a plant location. Although he would be losing a good worker, the manager realized that this employee's skills and enjoyment in relating to people suited him for personnel work. He nominated him for the position, and the employee became a capable and very motivated personnel assistant.

Individual work values. What is perceived as being of worth in employees' work lives is as varied as their talents. Whereas one engineer in the package design section may have a sense of accomplishment in successfully completing any project, another engineer may be motivated by an artistic desire to add to the esthetics of an avant-garde product. An effective manager takes these different work values into consideration when assigning projects.

A manager should be aware of the particular area of concern in an individual's work and his basic perceptions toward working as a whole. One person may be motivated by a desire for self-vested power or importance in the eyes of others, while another may be sincerely dedicated to the improvement of society through his job. The latter individual may be frustrated and unproductive in a position where he sees no real social benefit in his work.

Past job experiences. An employee's past job experiences influence his present motivation. It is unwise to assign a project requiring great imagination to an employee who recently has experienced failures. He may be gun-shy, unsure of his own ability, psychologically preparing himself for another failure, and he may not be able to put his all into an assignment. At the same time, by using the supportive approach with a person whose self-assurance needs a lift, a manager can give his employee a chance to prove himself through an important assignment.

Awareness of a person's job history of successes and failures, as well as the other bench marks of motivation—expectation of job content, work interests, abilities, and work values—will enable a manager to release motivated effort from his staff and help him avoid emotionally costly, time-consuming, involved problems resulting from misplaced, dissatisfied employees.

Layer Two

The next layer in our motivation pyramid is an awareness of the perceptions each individual brings to his work. Before starting a job, every employee has certain preconceptions about his work and what he expects for his own growth and job satisfaction. Often, prior conceptions do not agree with the realities of the job.

After four years at XYZ Corporation in general accounting, Mr. Smith is ready to tackle his first managerial job. He has decided to join a larger corporation that seemed impressed with his achievements, his deep-rooted growth goals, and his sophisticated mathematics background. In turn, he is eager to turn his energies loose, giving them practical release in the management profession. He can hardly wait to get his teeth into some of those exciting corporate growth projects described in his job interview, and he anticipates that his controller will seek his advice.

After five months Smith has done little more than glorified clerical work in preparing reports. His suggestions for improving the corporate long-range planning functions and reporting procedures have met with a cold reception, and his ideas for improving planning and budgeting are either ignored or misinterpreted. Disappointed and frustrated, Smith puzzles over changing jobs, letting off steam to his controller, or asking for a new assignment. Both he and his controller are dissatisfied.

In Smith's case, motivation is almost nonexistent because of the disparity between his job expectations and what he is actually doing. Furthermore, his boss is equally frustrated, not understanding what went wrong with his selected, dedicated, new manager. The motivation gap is enormous; there is no combination of personal expectations and perceived job elements.

In some instances, such as the above, the incompatibility between expectations and job realities—for both employer and employee—could be remedied by what we call MBCO (management by clear objectives). If an employee is made aware, and regularly updated throughout his job, of exactly what is expected of him, he is less likely to infer erroneous perceptions about the purpose of his work, his position in the organization, and his particular contribution.

If Smith's controller had clearly defined his duties, and explained why his first few months would be filled with many rudimentary, often unstimulating assignments, Smith would have had far more accurate psychological preconditioning for his job and thus might have experienced less frustration. After establishing and describing realistic job needs and attainable goals for Smith, his boss could then have indicated how a particular assignment—which might appear to be unnecessary or beneath his talents—fitted into the total picture.

Just as Smith's boss could have scored higher in the practice of expectation clarity, he could have further enhanced his new manager's motivations with appreciation. This would include not only sincerely complimenting Smith's handling of a particular assignment but also giving him a boost in handling any new job difficulties.

As a final comment, it should be remembered that MBCO is not limited to the positive aspects of mutual goal setting and performance appreciation. Observing and constructive coaching and counseling can go a long way toward motivation support. When given honestly and backed by hard performance data, such advice convinces an employee of his boss's true concern about his performance. Without such coaching, an employee labors under the notion that his work is completely acceptable, and Robert Louis Stevenson's observation, that "the cruellest lies are often told in silence," becomes a living truth. Only after being passed over for a promotion or denied a salary raise will an employee realize that his performance was not satisfactory. At this point, the motivation gap is painful.

Layer Three

The next layer is the utilitarian value of the work itself, as perceived by the employee. Motivation release has a direct relation to the amount of good the employee sees in the work. Value is in the eyes of the employee, not in the eyes of his boss.

It is becoming increasingly difficult for some military products companies to recruit or even to interview students. Student antiwar sentiments motivate them to reject a position with a company responsible for producing war instruments. Likewise, the recent uproars over the threatened environment have put many companies on the blacklist. Some studies indicate that there is an observable increase over the past few years in graduates entering the academic and government sectors of employment. Apparently, college graduates' increasing interest in highly meaningful and "goodness" goals is responsible for this trend. There is now a search for employment that provides the feeling that the end products are worthy of one's personal effort.

Awareness that concern for public welfare may be a job-motivating factor is necessary. Such awareness will enable a manager to understand why an individual may be more motivated to assist in retraining the hard-core unemployed or the disadvantaged than to be in a marketing or financial position.

A second dimension of the layer of utilitarian value is the goodness of the job as the individual perceives it in relation to himself. Besides being relevant to his desire to significantly contribute, a job needs to complement an individual's self-concept. In other words, to release the motivation mileage from within an employee, managers have the opportunity to convey to an employee a sense of the importance of his contribution and how he is of greater worth to himself through his job contributions.

In his novel *House of the Dead,* the 19th-century Russian novelist Dostoevski stated, "If it were desired to reduce a man to nothing, it would be necessary only to give his work a character of uselessness." The most crucial position can be ignored or degraded to the point of appearing useless, and, conversely, routine performance tasks can be elevated to a position of pride by management's sensitivity to the influences of the job on a man's view of himself. One of the ablest managers we have encountered continually impressed on her employees the vital nature of their work. "We are the guts of this whole building and of the company," she used to say. "Every major report, every sales promotion brochure, every bulletin or new policy report comes out of our department. If we miss deadlines, if we are sloppy or inaccurate, we are letting the whole company down, but, more important, we are disgracing ourselves as human beings." Each member of her staff, from typists to copy machine operators, performed with concern, care, and a sense of their own importance. Thus each person's self-concept was expanded and complemented through the work itself, and motivation was released through each individual's sense of his own value and critical importance.

Layer Four

Motivational release exists in direct proportion to the degree of association one feels with his job. Yet what about the person on the company payroll who seems detached, uninterested, and dissatisfied? What can a manager do, in addition to reexamining the person's particular interests, skills, work values, and personality needs, to further support and release his motivations?

Our suggestion is to cultivate the three Bs in each employee: to belong, to be, and to become.

To belong . . . to be group-accepted. An employee's sense of company and job belonging is enriched if he feels that others in the group are aware of the importance of his job. Although personal recognition by one's manager is vital and meaningful, group acceptance is also important for job motivational release.

It is wise, then, when introducing a new employee to his co-employees, to explain the significance of what the new person is contributing and how his work relates to the others'. This can be done in such a way that the regular employee is boosted by the boss's public compliment on his contribution and the new employee gains familiarity with the department as a whole and with his own part in the group's achievements.

Such an approach does not go unnoticed by a new employee or by anyone else in the department. Even the seemingly nonchalant or thick-skinned employee is sensitive when it comes to manager and group acceptance of the importance of the various work stations within the department.

To be . . . a somebody. Every person, whether company president or office janitor, has a notion of what he himself is, first, as a person and second, as an employee. Each person is searching through his work life for ways to further his sense of identity and self-meaningfulness.

An individual expects to be treated in a manner consistent with the picture he has of himself. Going back to our Mr. Smith, we see that one of the initial problems he encountered was a discrepancy in the way in which he was treated by his manager and the way he felt he deserved to be treated, that is, as he saw himself and his capabilities. Through his job, he wanted to achieve self-fulfillment by using his academic background and work consciousness. Yet he was not treated in accordance with his self-image but rather as an inexperienced, overzealous youth. Such managerial insensitivity detracted from his self-image; not only did his motivation decrease but his self-confidence as well.

By considering the "to be" aspect of this employee's self-image his manager could have gauged his particular assignments more carefully. In addition, he could have presented assignments that Smith considered beneath him or mechanical in such a way that their meaningfulness would be apparent.

To become . . . to fulfill one's capabilities. Each of us not only has an image of what he is at present but also a desire to go beyond this—to develop and grow in self-worth. The German poet Goethe expressed concisely how the need "to become" is released in each individual: "If you treat a man as he is, he will remain as he is. But if you treat him as if he were what he ought to be and could be, he will become what he ought to be and could be." Such a motivational prescription seems obvious, but too few supervisors follow it. By determining and encouraging a man's potential, a manager does more to make a man "become" than if he tried to change his weak points.

Many times people are aware of their own talents and are eager to experiment with developing those skills and abilities, particularly if their manager encourages them to become what they are capable of becoming. But, as in the example of the market research employee who became a personnel assistant, it is quite possible that an individual may have additional potential and special abilities. Here a manager who observes an employee at close range many hours a week can be of developmental assistance. In this case the manager made a decision that meant losing the employee's skills in his department. This does not always have to be the case. Often, the manager can also help his department "to become" by developing an individual through varied assignments. The employee's increased contribution will enhance the department's productivity and quality.

A few final remarks are in order about the ways managers can destroy the three Bs in employees. One supervisory abuse is giving an employee a useless assignment. A second is leaving room for little or no job content determination on the part of an employee. The manager who assigns a report and then dictates everything, from the format to the conclusion to the steps necessary to reach that conclusion, is making a motivational error. An assignment left to an employee's own design may initially take longer to complete than it would if the manager gives step-by-step directions. Yet by using his own ingenuity in performing the assignment, the individual is more closely associated with the next work task—and perhaps may come up with new ways to improve it.

Falling short in job appreciation or using humiliation as a negative motivation approach or leadership style are other ways. Finally, the manager who projects lack of confidence in a person, thinking that this will be an impetus to motivate him, is actually reversing the entire three Bs process. By treating a man as less than he is, a manager creates a climate of demotivation and apathy; he promotes an attitude of "I don't need to try my hardest because he doesn't expect that much of me anyway."

Better that a manager build and continually surround his employees with a climate for excellence, an expectation of the very best from each one. In this kind of atmosphere the three Bs flourish and develop; productive, meaningful work is accomplished.

Layer Five

The final supportive layer in the motivation pyramid is each individual's need to feel important. Do you make your employees feel important when they are in your office, or do you try to make yourself feel important?

How does a manager generate a feeling of personal and job importance within his employees? We suggest that a person's sense of importance is directly related to the influence he feels that he has in his work. Thus, by establishing multiple opportunities for a man to exercise influence, a manager is going a long way in helping this individual to feel important.

Furthermore, each manager should be aware of the "influence compass," that is, the different directions that an employee's opportunity to influence can include.

Due north. A manager can instill a sense of job and personal importance in an employee by being receptive to an employee's influence (suggestions) and giving an employee the chance to influence upward. Make your interest known by directly soliciting his advice. Give full attention to someone who has come up with a new idea. A manager's sincere willingness to spend his time intently listening to an employee is an indication of the importance he accords that person.

Another way a manager encourages upward influence is to let an employee influence the big boss: "Frank, I read your report this morning at our meeting with the vice president of sales. He was very interested in your ideas for increasing profits in our southern branch and I would like you to get together with him to explain your recommendations more fully."

Due east, due west. A manager can motivate an employee by letting him influence sideward; that is, be allowing him to deal freely with members of other departments, letting him sit in on their meetings, and so forth. It is usually enough to say, "Nick, I need this matter straightened out in the other department. Please represent us. Handle it as you judge best and requisition any help you need."

Due south. Equally important, a supervisor should have the opportunity to influence downward, that is, to manage his own subordinates without interference from his boss. Not only is this vital to his own supervisory concept and self-importance, it is also necessary to gain respect from his own staff. Details, such as whether a man's secretary deserves a raise, when his staff should take vacations, and so forth, should be left to him.

Due center. Finally, and a salient key for job identification, a man should be able to influence and give meaning to his own work. Robert Louis Stevenson said,: "Give me the man with brains enough to make a fool of himself." Although Stevenson hit on the less positive aspect of this freedom to influence self, his point is well taken. True job motivation includes not only the opportunity to initiate new ideas and make decisions but occasionally to make some errors as well. The motivated employee can only profit by these occasional mistakes. Because the task was his baby, so to speak, he will take the responsibility for the error and see that it is not repeated. Also, recognizing the freedom he has been given and the trust his manager has invested in him, he will commit his efforts to the job because the boss's job has become his job.

Performance without signs of approval is like winking at a pretty girl in the dark; you know what you're doing, but no one else does. Although performance should receive both monetary and verbal acknowledgment of a job well done, recognition is the more necessary of the two. A person should be paid commensurate with his performance, yet a silent raise each year contributes little toward an employee's feeling of job identification. Far more necessary to his peace of mind and self-esteem is the acknowledgment of a job well done.

Many organization problems stem from management's inability to cope with different kinds of people, and from its failure to realize the complexities of employee motivation. Many successful businessmen and company managers are very profit oriented and this is their major concern. This is certainly a powerful attribute in management personnel. Yet it is becoming increasingly evident that if organized business, as we know it, is to be effective, our managers need to be more people oriented and become releasers of motivation from within each employee.

Layer Six

A salient point for release of drive and commitment is the establishment of a climate for real achievement and responsibility. Ultimately, the elements we have explored—job perception, personal and social meaningfulness of work, the three Bs—mesh and interact together, resulting in a situation conducive to achievement through psychological association with one's work. What are some marks of this fertile type of achievement climate and how is this climate facilitated by managers?

Mutual goal setting. One mark of an achieving climate is the establishment of mutually determined goals—a direct outgrowth of our stress on MBCO. A manager should clearly define his goals and mutually outline with an employee what is expected of him. When this approach is combined with an awareness of an individual's personality needs and his need to participate in the degrees of the influence compass, we have a situation in which job objectives are alive and relevant to both the employee and his manager.

A manager needs to develop with his employee realistic, well-defined task goals that call for real contribution, not busy work. The atmosphere between the two should be open with no hidden job achievement expectations on either side.

Defined responsibilities. Only by taking into consideration a person's particular talents, job interests, and goals can a manager determine in what way a man's potential will best be put to use, and delegate the authority to make decisions, to act, and to make commitments. Once the goals are set and the areas of his authority delineated, the employee is ready to meet these goals in ways he feels are most effective. His job climate is such that he has freedom to manage and direct his efforts without interference. He likewise has the job freedom and the manager's confidence to take certain risks and to commit time, money, and human resources in these areas of responsibility.

Shared power. In conjunction with clarification of responsibility and authority is shared power, a marriage of trust between supervisor and employee. Neither side is secretive or surreptitious in methods or objectives. Of course, when an employee is given authority to decide on a course of action, his manager is entitled to periodic progress reports. Just as a marriage is a contract between two consenting and motivated adults, so also is the employee–manager relationship a type of mutual sharing of power agreement between two adults, surrounded by a trustful, productive relationship.

Results expectations. A motivating achievement climate is charged with results expectation. A manager expects high standards and affirmative, effective results, not just an appearance of activity and being busy. Willa Cather, a colorful and prolific writer of pioneer America, once made the tongue-in-cheek observation that "we like people who do things, even if we only see their faces on a cigar box lid." Such an observation holds true in business. A brilliant new product or a workable method to cut costs may not come every day, but in the day-to-day situation, it is the employee who produces results who is effective. A wise manager not only recognizes these results, but continually encourages them, expects them, and rewards them. Motivation is stimulated in a climate of expected excellence of performance and the reward of results.

Employee benefits. The employee who has been involved in an achieving environment reflects an ability to act toward clearly established goals, and he is able to review his own progress and continually assess his own performance in achieving the objectives. As he gets further into the assignment, he periodically can develop a project progression checklist on himself—a performance balance sheet containing his own job debits and credits.

Manager benefits. On the other side of personal project control and monitoring, the manager who has provided the logistic support to his employees also benefits from the self-motivating climate. The more effective the staff is, the stronger is the manager's position. A manager who firmly supports his men and who shares his power has instigated a motivation climate. He gives of his power and his influence and, in return, is supported by the achievements and accomplishments of his staff.

The climate for achievement is characterized by three bench marks: (1) the manager's communicated, firm belief in employee responsibility for visible, significant achievements; (2) the mutual goal setting and concern of both manager and employee for the measured progression of projects against standards of excellence; and (3) the shared and delegated power among personnel. Both sides reap the benefits through task accomplishment.

Layer Seven

If managers are to assist employees in coming to life through their work, such as in George Bernard Shaw's play, *Pygmalion,* then one of the motivational release mechanisms is a person's self-concept and the treatment of an individual equal to one's self-image. As Professor Higgins said, "The difference between a lady and a flower girl is not how she behaves, but how she is treated." Employees are motivated when their managers *see* them, *treat* them, and *communicate* to them as capable of performance excellence.

People vibrate negatively when confronted by a manager's statement, "Who the heck do you think you are?" People have a notion of who they are as individuals and as employees; the key point is, are you treating and approaching your employees through their self-perception, or are your behaviors and work assignments demeaning and infringing upon their view of themselves?

Assignments and the nature of the work itself become challenging and motivating when they are equal to a person's self-perceived abilities and self-worth. Conversely, assignments lose their motivational appeal when they are employee-perceived as below one's self-estimated ability, dignity, and training-experience backgrounds. Our suggestion is that the apex of the motivational pyramid is casting assignments and allocating work in terms of the employee's calibration of his self-worth compared with the essence of the assignment. When presented with an assignment from their manager, employees ask themselves, "Is this project worthy of me?" not, "Am I worthy of this task?"

The work itself and the way in which it is assigned are psychologically gauged by the employee in terms of his self-image—who he is, and who he is not. Are your employees increasing their self-respect through the work they are asked to perform? When they can see an increase in self-respect and self-worth through their relationship to the job and through their relationship with their manager, motivation is released from within and the employee can identify more closely with his department. A key point for motivation release is the employee's measure of the job against who he is, and wants to be, as a human being.

As a final comment, consider the following quote from Thomas Wolfe, a perceptive critic of our times:

If a man has a talent and cannot use it, he has failed. If he has a talent and learns somehow to use it, he has gloriously succeeded and has won a satisfaction and a triumph few men ever know.

This "learns somehow" is the motivational domain of managers today. We suggest that the key to "somehow" is the release of motivation from within the employee. The challenge of today's managers is to manage this complex force by establishing an achievement climate.

11

Preventing Credibility Gaps

How often have you heard something like this in your organization: "The trouble is no one will fire the incompetents. The management people don't back you up. If there were just some way to get through to these people around here, the company would be in better shape and the shop would operate a lot more smoothly."

Such remarks usually come from the "suffering-attitude manager." No matter where you go in corporate life, no matter where you are in the hierarchy of a particular company, you find this long-suffering type. He realizes that he is getting less than top performance from his people, and he points out to those around him that the failings of his department are due to the lack of support he receives from marginal people who work there. He almost seems to enjoy this self-flagellation.

No manager can get more performance out of a group than the group is motivated to give. Employees are the most important of the manager's resources. They are the tools that help him get a job done. People can develop, can add to their knowledge and understanding, can learn new and better ways of doing things. Thus it is vital that a manager know how to talk, and listen, direct, and involve his employees if he is to achieve growth of their net worth. Through coaching and counseling of employees, it is possible to get superior performance from the capable employee as well as to get through to the problem employee.

In many companies the coaching and counseling process is thought of as a once-a-year appraisal or performance-evaluation procedure. At such times the boss gets together with the employee and tells him what he thinks of the man's performance. All year long the man dreads the coming event. The employee is called in, pulled up short, and told where he has messed up all year or where he has done a good job. In either case, he is unable to do anything about it because it is all ancient history. According to research done on this subject, any praise given at this time is generally discounted as simple window dressing in which is hidden the raw meat of criticism.

Another interesting finding is that employees respond defensively to a year's supply of criticism. Apparently, there is an overloading factor that prevents people from handling a great deal of criticism all at once. In light of all of the negative connotations and consequences of the annual after-the-fact appraisal, it is obvious that evaluation and measurement against objectives should be an ongoing process. Employees need regular feedback about their performance. They need to have frequent input about their ability to handle their job.

A number of organizations are moving toward a work planning and review system in which work objectives for the coming period are agreed to by both the employee and the boss. At regularly scheduled meetings, the objectives themselves are reviewed (for adequacy and accuracy), and the man's evolving needs and progress toward meeting objectives are reviewed. Most important about this approach is the fact that it not only removes the sting of the annual performance appraisal but it tends to be job-centered rather than personality-centered. In management, results are what we are really concerned with. We want achievement, not psychotherapy. We are not interested in changing personalities or attitudes, except as these affect achievement by the work unit. Therefore, a system based on accomplishment of work objectives is more central and more accurate than concern about personality quirks. When work planning and review sessions are not personality-centered but work-centered, the employee is able to stand apart from his own performance and analyze it more objectively.

We should point out that processes and procedures are not central to the basic question, which is the *relationship* that should exist between the supervisor and the subordinate. No paper system is ever going to improve a person's performance or adequately assess that performance if the relationship between him and his boss does not facilitate communication. Our central concern in the coaching and counseling process is people, not procedures; employees, not processes; human beings, not paperwork.

Many things interfere with the development of open and authentic communication. The time constraint is one. A lot of running around has to be done. A manager has to manage. He has to remove organization barriers, he has to answer the phone, and so forth. Coaching and counseling are a time-consuming process. How can you possibly take time out of your schedule to do it?

If you are to get a return on your investment from the people in your unit, then the key to that goal is to *get through to them.* If you constantly make efforts to get through to the other person, to communicate with him, to understand him, then he will have less anxiety and you will have less tension in your relations with him. There will then be the possibility that your employees will work with determination and motivation instead of going into retirement while they are still on the job.

As a manager, you have been cursed with a title. Before getting into management, we are inclined to think of the title as a goal to be achieved. But in terms of interpersonal communications, or getting through to another individual, the title often acts as a barrier. If you start issuing orders and edicts and commands because you have a title, then you will turn people off and they will tune out your needs, desires, and ambitions. They may sabotage you, work against you, be noncommittal; or they may conform fearfully. There are many "lifers" in organizations—people who simply draw their pay, who, in essence, have turned their minds off and are going through the motions of the job without commitment. It is a frightening way to live, but employees do adopt these tactics as a way to survive. It is interesting to think of the vast numbers of people in companies who are acting like old-timers at age 38 to 48, who are simply there drawing their pay.

But, you say, "What can I do to get them to go back to work? How can I help them to make a commitment? What can I do to help them feel some job satisfaction and have a sense of accomplishment from the job? How can I get productive activity from these people?"

The following suggestions detail some of the ways toward these goals. But remember that the mechanics of counseling and coaching—the techniques and skills involved—are all secondary in importance to your attitude and your goal. You must keep in mind why you are there and what you want to achieve through the coaching process.

EXCHANGE IDEAS AND PERCEPTIONS FOR CREDIBILITY

Each of us looks at a situation differently, forming our own immediate perceptions of what is happening and what the facts are. We lock very quickly into our own stereotypes and impressions of what is involved. One executive vice president was described as having a mind like concrete—all mixed up and permanently set.

It is easy to see how we get locked into our judgment patterns. A lot of second-guessing goes on in organization living, a lot of nonsense that says," I understand this guy, and I understand what is going wrong with his operations. Believe me, when I call him in I'm going to tell him exactly what he's doing wrong and what he should do differently." For a manager to go into a session with an employee with that preset attitude spells disaster. Viewing oneself as having absolute authority is an attitude that spells trouble. Try to picture the interview in advance— the way you will sit, the way you will act, intonations of your voice. It is by these cues that the subordinate surmises your attitude. He may perceive he is in for real trouble, deserved or not. Your mind is made up, and there is no court of appeal; what is in store for him is a kangaroo court.

While you are trying to picture the interview situation, think of the last time you were called into your executive's office and placed under the same pressures. You were probably wondering why he didn't give you a chance to tell him what really happened. An attitude of being primed to talk *at* a man, of being ready to ream him out but not to listen to him, is extremely destructive to work relationships.

It is so obvious that it is a shame to even have to say it, but one should go into these sessions with an attitude of exchanging ideas and perceptions. The word "interview" literally means an exchange of views—an "inter-viewing" between two people. Sometimes these sessions are approached with preconceived ideas because we feel that it is time to reinforce the image of being *boss*. Some executives achieve a false sense of security by reinforcing the image of their greatness in the minds of those who cower before them. They sit behind their desk—which reminds people of their status and authority—rather than openly trying to understand their subordinates' points of view. The purpose of coaching and counseling is to sit with the other human being and try to honestly understand him and honestly understand the situation—not to act as judge and jury.

A second objective of these sessions is to facilitate performance as best we can—that is, to modify a man's actions. However, before we can modify behavior we must first understand the man and the situation. He must have the feeling that we really do understand. He must be willing and ready to say to himself, "From what you're saying and from the way you're acting toward me, it's obvious you have an interest in knowing me and my views. You really do want to know." If he really has that impression of you, he will open up and tell you what he thinks. But if he thinks you are nodding in three-quarter time, saying yes once every 60 seconds—if your attitude is "I've got to listen to you; I read that in a book somewhere"—then your employee is going to approach this one-way process defensively. He will sit there playing the defensive games that are necessary to protect himself from the offensive games you are playing. A battle of wits ensues, and the whole objective of change of performance is forgotten.

REMOVE THE TENSION

For a person to want to change his performance effectiveness, he has to want to commit himself to new standards. Whenever you have been called into the "old man's" office, you have probably experienced a moment of tension. Many questions run through your mind, and a jolt goes through your emotional system. It is very important to remember that experience, because now *you* are the old man in the eyes of your employees and they see *you* as the one who raises this anxiety in them. You are the one who emotionally elevates or downgrades them. You are the one who has a great impact on their future.

When the employee comes into your office he knows that you are trying to determine something. He will come into the situation vigilant and with his guard up. He will hear what he wants to hear and see what he wants to see. He may go through some superficial movements and words to get you off his back, and he may, if he is talented, give you some razzle-dazzle. Second-guessing has already started. No real communication takes place, and little will be done about changing his on-the-job behavior. His primary goal is to "psych" out of the session as quickly as possible because it makes him uncomfortable. For him the goal is not to act or be different on the job. His goal is, in whatever way possible, to squirm out or bale out of the situation as he can.

Before you can communicate, you must get past these barriers. You have to remove the emotional set that blocks you out. This may mean that you will have to let him explode and vent all his doubts, fears, hostilities, and anxieties. This skill of being an emotional sponge is not in your job description. The abuse, suspicion, and fear that is directed your way is one of the callings of supervision. For your effectiveness, for your visibility, for your mutual advantage in getting the job done, it is important that your people are talking *with* you and not playing *at* you. However, if the employee is going to identify with his job, if he is going to identify with *you*, he must have a safe opportunity to blow his stack. Some hostility may be directed at you in the form of abuse. But if you take it as a personal affront, he is going to sense this is a very tender spot with you, a managerial Achilles' heel. Either he will never be able to fully and honestly communicate with you because he knows you cannot enter into that kind of confronting relationship, or he will leave your office smiling because he now knows how to get to you. To be effective, it is important that your people talk to you, not at you. Therefore, be genuine and let the person get all the negative feelings out of his system. Just sit there and take it before giving him your input.

Those of you who were exposed to the interesting experience of military service may recall one of the first lessons you were taught: to do reconnaissance before you went charging up a hill. You never knew with certainty what was over the hill. The same lesson applies to coaching sessions. Although you may assume that the employee coming to see you isn't loaded for bear and is unprepared emotionally, he may, in fact, come in loaded with heavy armament. He may be ready to control the session so he can "win." We describe the situation as if it were competitive—you versus him. This may very well be his perception. One of your managerial goals is to remove the tension before trying to counsel the employee.

IDENTIFY BARRIERS
TO PERFORMANCE

Do you really understand what is causing the problem when an employee is having difficulty in achieving a job objective? Many times logistics barriers or operating concerns may prevent him from doing the job well. Perhaps you assume the barrier is within the person himself: the man is a goof-off, he is lazy, he has a "care-less" attitude. But you may be mistaken. True, there are incompetent, lazy people in organizations who fail because of their own ineptness. There are marginal and submarginal performers, those who perhaps should be reassigned or terminated. But if we walk into the counseling session with such a preconceived attitude about the performance problem, convinced that the employee is motivationally low, we could be making a tragic, prejudicial mistake. One of the objectives of the counseling session is to try to ascertain the other's point of view. This is an effective way to manage and to build a relationship: identify this person's needs, his operating problems, and the stones that lie in his path.

GET RESULTS WITH PEOPLE

It used to be that one of the badges of honor of a supervisor was his ability to quote the rules and regulations; the rules and the labor contract were a way to maintain control. Imagine what that approach produces in a counseling situation, in which the employee has some legitimate barriers or grievances. Do you do nothing more than remind the man of company policy or recite the rules? Are you so insecure that you have to demonstrate your inalienable power and rights?

In our understanding of management, it is clear that the manager's role is to function as a human being first, rather than as a bureaucratic tin god devoid of feeling and concern. Some people believe that this statement represents soft management and capitulation to subordinates. But we have seen strong, solid managers functioning first as human beings. One of the ways to increase your chances and odds in the management game is to function in terms of how you feel about an individual. You have to put feelings into supervision! It is important to be genuine in that session with the person, not a role player. You don't have to treat him like a child and recite all the rules. He doesn't have to be reminded of the impact you can have on his life, of the power you have. What he really wants to know is whether you have the ability to meet him as an equal and listen to him.

A key question about the coaching and counseling session is, "Are you after *con*formance or are you after *per*formance?" If you are after conformance, then all you have to do is remind him you are the boss and of his subordinate relationship to you. But to achieve performance, you are going to have to mutually agree that you have a job to do. It is the opportunity to say to the person that if only we would work together, maybe together the two of us could cut it—this is the core of manager credibility.

APPRAISAL FEEDBACK

We have yet to meet a person in organizations who wouldn't like to know how he stands, how he is doing, and whether his boss thinks he is going anywhere in his career. Everyone wants to know whether he is in favor with the boss or whether the boss sees him as nothing more than a well-paid pair of hands. How does he see your performance? Is he aware that you are doing a job? Does he recognize that you have problems? If he does, where is the recognition? "The problem with this company," many persons say, "is that nobody knows what I'm doing. The only man who knows how well I'm doing is too busy to tell me." Does that sound familiar?

Scott Myers used the following situation to illustrate this point. Suppose you were to be in a bowling competition, with a $100 prize to the one with the highest score. To make things interesting, a curtain is halfway down the alley so that the bowlers can't see the pins or the scoreboard. The experiment shows that an adult can bowl for about three frames but then becomes frustrated in not knowing how he is doing. And yet, every day in organization life, people roll the ball and knock down the pins, but do not get any feedback. It is an unpleasant feeling and it causes a lot of frustration. Give your man regular, current, and honest feedback on how you see his work and what your expectations of him are.

REACH AGREEMENT

Management should communicate clear performance expectations to the employee because we all tend to drift into low-producing and low-impact activities. These projects are comfortable, generally producing little anxiety or tension. In an area where we cannot get into trouble, we find safety and a feeling of job security. However, this drifting is getting off the track. In such situations, coaching sessions will reinforce your expectations with the employee. Here you have an opportunity to correct any wrong impressions, change his task images, and agree on mutual expectations.

Counseling sessions are a time for agreement and comparative assessment, where actual performance is compared with management's expectations. Many times this can be a pleasant, reinforcing experience for the employee, depending on the degree to which his performance has matched expected standards. But it need not be a time when all is well and the emphasis is on happiness. Sometimes the person is not getting certain jobs done. These variations in his performance must be discussed, even to the point where this involves negative feelings. The core of human relations is that you are for real as a person and can share your pride and disappointment with others.

Most important is where you put the emphasis in getting the other person to understand what you expect. Some managers go into a coaching session with the self-oriented, godlike attitude that they have to charge this guy up, they have to change his personal behavior. The other side of the coin is that the person wants to do the job, he wants to overcome the obstacles, but he needs clarification and supervisory help. He has a family and all the accompanying responsibility. He *wants* to do the job. Regardless of the underlying reasons for his behavior, you as a manager must sit down and talk about your expectations so that he can be effective.

Don't make anyone try to second-guess you and have to wonder what the old man really wants. Get to the point and tell him what the situation is as you see it. Any other way is playing games. This is what human relations is, this is what coaching and counseling are—letting him know what you do and do not want him to do.

An illustration of this point was given to us by a consultant. In a certain power company, he was working with the general manager, who called him in and said, "I want you to give me the latest black magic on how to fire someone. You should be able to tell me how to tie the can to my controller." When asked, "What do you want from the controller and what don't you want?" the general manager said, "He is doing everything I don't want him to do and he is not doing the things I expected he would do." The consultant said, "Why don't you tell me what you expect of him?" For about an hour and a half the general manager paced up and down and spelled out very specifically what he expected of this man and what he wanted him to stop doing.

That afternoon the controller invited the consultant into his office and said, "I've wanted to talk to you for some time. I have a problem with the general manager. I can't seem to please him on anything." The consultant said, "I was talking to your general manager this morning and he told me there was some dissatisfaction between the two of you." The controller responded, "That's the understatement of the year. That man is making me climb the wall. I just don't understand what he wants me to do." Said the consultant, "Well, this morning he told me clearly his expectations for you. I wrote it all down." The controller asked to see it. "Heck, no!" was the answer; "I am an ethical consultant. I cannot violate the privacy of the session."

After establishing the ethic under which he operates, the consultant said, "I have to go to the library and it will take me about an hour and a half to do my research and reading." He left his notes on the controller's desk. When the consultant returned, the papers were still hot from the copying machine!

Four months later the consultant was back in the same plant. The general manager said, "Hey, you really know how to communicate. You did a great job; here's your check." "It is very nice to receive it, but I am here to tell you I am here to resign." The general manager said, "What do you mean you are going to resign? You are doing a job for us." The consultant said, "The only employee we talked about last time is still on the payroll and it is because of him that I am going to resign. I violated one of my professional ethics. I told him what you told me in our private session. Remember you told me exactly what you wanted this guy to stop doing and exactly what you wanted him to start doing. Not only did I tell him, I showed him in writing." He thought a minute and said, "You know, now I know what I've been doing wrong; I have not been explicit in my expectations."

Be specific about what you want on the job. If you want people to run in a horse race, you have to tell them which track to run on. Otherwise, they will go to the wrong track and run in the wrong race. They will be unhappy and you will be unhappy. You both lose! Your employees must clearly know what they are to do, what the goals are. You can tell them participatively, you can do it autocratically, you can do it kindly, you can do it directly. The technique is up to you. There is no corner on wisdom in this area as to exactly how you do it. But when your employee walks out of that session, he must walk out knowing what your expectations are for him. And you will hopefully have gained some feedback from him in terms of how he perceives his own objectives in that particular job.

GET RIGHT TO THE PROBLEM

Textbooks on coaching tell you to establish rapport as the first step in the counseling session, that it is appropriate to have an initial warm-up and some conversation. But the employee sitting on the other side of the desk is saying to himself, "The old man knows why I am here. He is going to say something to me. Why doesn't he get over the preliminaries and tell me what he wants." Our suggestion is that you get to the point immediately. It is important that you retain control of the first part of the conversation. You can most effectively have that control by making a clear statement of why you are together. This is not the time to wait for him to betray himself when you hit a nerve. Let him know where you stand and what you perceive. Ask for his responses, his story, hear his thoughts on the situation. He may have some additional information that you don't. You want him to fill that gap, to fill in information and perceptions you don't have, whether he gives them to you in a biased form or not. Your goal is to reach agreement and a plan of action.

We would like to reemphasize the necessity of letting him vent his feelings and emotions, not only to achieve positive interpersonal feelings, but also to insure the effectiveness of the session in terms of planned problem solution. If he comes out of that session uptight and silent, then you have failed. Think back to some of the sessions you have had with your boss where he failed you, where it seemed quite clear that he had his mind made up and had drawn his conclusions before you even came in. He never heard you. He just wanted you to say "Yes, Sir" and go quietly. The next time you face the employee who works with you, remember how you felt in his shoes.

WINNING TOGETHER
PRODUCES CREDIBILITY

Coaching and counseling constitute a key management task. As a boss, you still want to be able to lead based on the soundness of your relationship. You know that if you yell at them and give them a hard time you will be uncomfortable with them. To function effectively, you will need zest or gusto in working with people to enhance their ability to contribute. And to enhance behavior, you are going to have to facilitate their wanting to do something differently. The person has to be convinced in his mind, not outthought or outshouted. He has to be committed to a need or reason for change. The buyer must want to buy if the sale is to be effective.

In part, we are saying that you must have the ability to say to the employee, "I need you. I need your contribution, I need your talent. You are a valued member of this team and *we must win together.*" If you do mean it and really feel that way, tell him so.

All of the attitudes and approaches in coaching and counseling happen because of the need to establish agreement to get the job done. It is not something that is done as a social ritual. It is not done to play games. Coaching and counseling happen because something needs to happen in the world of work. The subordinate knows he has a job to do but something has gotten out of whack. The manager has a series of expectations or criteria of performance he needs to have happen, and yet the subordinate is going down his own primrose path. If he continues, you have a real problem gap. This presents an opportunity for a coaching and counseling session because there is this gap. There is a variance between what is actually occurring and what is expected. There is a need for a counseling and coaching session in order to get the project back on target. Coaching and counseling can be an effective problem analysis tool in mutually solving some of the performance variations which are faced in management. Credibility results by an honest working together and mutually understanding each other through openness.

PART FOUR

THE MANAGER AS A PERSON

It is not the critic who counts, or how the strong man stumbled and fell, or where the doer of deeds could have done them better. The credit belongs to the man who is actually in the arena, whose face is marred by dust and sweat and blood, who strives valiantly, who errs and comes short again and again, who knows the great enthusiasms, the great devotion, and spends himself in a worthy cause; and if he fails, at least fails while daring greatly, so that he'll never be with those cold and timid souls who know neither victory nor defeat.

—*Theodore Roosevelt*

12

The Maturing
Manager

In a recent consultation, one of our clients, the president of an industrial corporation, said, "The primary question I ask myself in determining whether a man is fit for management responsibility is, 'Is this man mature?'" Maturity has come to be one of many criteria that separates those who are going somewhere in management from those who are not.

What is maturity? Many people equate maturity with mental ability or with chronological age. But maturity is not only a matter of intelligence or age or even training, education, or background.

Maturity is not a state of *being*. It is more a state of *becoming*. As Abraham Maslow, who has spent many years analyzing the healthy personality, pointed out, "The mature person wants to *be* the best he can be. In this area he has no competitors." The mature person does not try to emulate others but to fulfill himself. The emotionally mature person is not free from worry and difficulty. On the contrary, maturity is demonstrated by the way managers resolve their conflicts and the way they cope with problems. The mature person responds to difficulties positively and sees them as a challenge. As Mortimer Feinberg, the distinguished psychologist, said, the mature person is appropriately worried at times, but he is not crushed or defeated by his worries.

Technical competence, intelligence, and drive are important but not sufficient. People need the emotional maturity to work effectively by themselves and to deal constructively with others while under pressure. Many employees do a good job in ordinary circumstances but fall apart when the going gets rough. In the face of severe or unexpected problems, they panic, make rash decisions, withdraw from others, work compulsively on inconsequentials, scatter their efforts so widely as to be ineffective, and become aggressive toward others rather than directing their energies toward the task.

How does the mature person think and act? The essential elements of managerial maturity include the following.

SELF-KNOWLEDGE

"Know thyself" was a prime tenet of Greek philosophy. Without accurate knowledge of himself, the manager is handicapped in dealing effectively with the world at large or in handling his interpersonal relationships. Self-knowledge precedes self-mastery. The mature individual takes the time to make a personal inventory. He knows what his strengths and weaknesses are, and thus is free from the frustration of trying to be what he is not. Dr. Mortimer Feinberg, president of BFS Psychological Associates, observed that the mature manager sees things as they are, not as they might have been or as he wishes them to be.

How do you accept new challenges and responsibilities? How do you face reality? In discussions with others, are you willing to reexamine the assumptions you have always taken for granted? Are you open and divergent or closed and convergent in your thinking? What are your defense mechanisms, and the biases and prejudices that affect your thought processes? Have you found out who you are as a person? The mature person has established a realistic relationship between his experience and himself. If you do not know yourself, you will be estranged from others. If one is out of touch with oneself, then one cannot touch others. The inability to communicate meaningfully leads to failure.

Ilya Ehrenburg, the Russian novelist, reported an interview that had been granted by the late Albert Einstein:

Once when I was talking to Einstein, he asked me, smiling, "How much is 2 × 2?" Startled, I said I had been taught that the answer was 4. "But what do you think yourself?" he asked. "Four," I replied timidly. He smiled again: "As for me, I don't know. It might be five. . . ."

The open-minded executive who knows himself will not shut himself off from all the possibilities life has to offer.

SELF-ACCEPTANCE

Most people find it easier to admit their strengths than to concede their weaknesses. The mature manager recognizes his deficiencies, but has learned to accept himself as he is. In this self-acknowledgment process false pride is stripped away and replaced by a form of humility that produces strength, not weakness.

Self-acceptance does not mean self-satisfaction. The mature executive is struggling for self-improvement so as to better fulfill his unique potential. As we have said, he does not want to imitate others, but to fulfill himself. It is at this stage that conformity ceases and individuality begins. The mature manager has learned to keep his perspective. He balances his strengths against his weaknesses, and does not fall into the trap of thinking he is better or worse than he actually is. While not complacent, he accepts what he cannot change; he does change what he can. The immature person, on the other hand, is illustrated by a poem:

The Centipede

A centipede was happy, quite,
Until a frog in fun
Said, "Pray, which leg comes after which?"
This raised her mind to such a pitch,
She lay distracted in the ditch,
Considering how to run.

The mature manager knows how to pace himself; he does not beat himself, nor does he wallow in the depths of self-despair and self-pity. He has learned to live at peace with himself.

Realities about oneself are always hard to accept. Because we have all experienced failures, and handle some situations awkwardly, many of us are not content with our lot and still have dreams that we have not yet given up. But the mature man puts things into proper focus and does not live in a fantasy world.

ACCEPTANCE OF OTHERS

An executive must function within the framework of other people's strengths, weaknesses, abilities, and deficiencies. He is mature enough to respect these differences and doesn't try to mold others into his own image. This does not mean that he is softheaded or overly softhearted. Although he accepts others as they are, he will not coddle them if their shortcomings interfere with overall goals. The mature executive can fire a person, but he does it for the right reasons. Acceptance of others, despite their faults, makes one able to criticize constructively without feeling guilty.

The immature manager constantly gropes for social acceptance from everyone. His goal is for everyone to like him. The mature person knows that you don't have to give in to all the whims of others to make them like you, that you don't have to have the approval of everyone in order to respect yourself.

Christ taught us that we should love others as we love ourselves. The fact is that you cannot love and accept another person until you have first learned to respect yourself. Accepting others also means acknowledging our dependency on them—mature dependency that is realistic and reciprocal. The mature person is able to acknowledge this interdependency. He knows that none of us becomes a giant solely because of his own capabilities; we must all stand on the shoulders of those below us for support.

The philosopher Martin Buber once described the immature person as one who establishes "I-it" relationships. In an immature relationship the other person becomes an "it," an object, something to be manipulated. Because of the mature person's willingness to accept and respect others, he establishes "I-thou" relationships. The word "thou" was carefully chosen to illustrate the importance of respect and reverence for another person. Relationships at this level occur as a dialogue between adults. Avoiding facades, the mature person communicates sincerely and makes real contact with others. The mature manager is unwilling to manipulate people. Feinberg stated that he builds bridges between people instead of driving wedges.

The mature employee is able to show genuine care and concern as an expression of his acceptance of another. The English language imprecisely defines what love means to the mature person. The greeks had three words to describe the different types of love: *eros,* a physical or sensual love; *philia,* a brotherly love; and *agape,* wonder, expectation, charity, a love that transforms. The mature person transforms the lives of those around him because he is able to accept people on an *agape* level.

ACCEPTANCE OF RESPONSIBILITY

Immature people cry out against life; their failures are always caused by someone else, luck is against them, the odds are never on their side. The mature individual recognizes and accepts the responsibilities and restrictions inherent in the situations in which he operates. The mature manager treats people or assignments with a sense of the trust placed in him; he adopts the role of a steward. He realizes that the resources and personnel at his disposal are entrusted to him and that to fulfill his stewardship he must enlarge on what he has been given.

Responsibility has been defined as an individual's personal commitment to the success of all activities with which he is associated. It is the zest to do or get done what ought to be done. Believing in Santa Claus or relying on luck, a superior, or anyone else to solve one's problems may be a sign of immaturity. Accepting personal responsibility is necessary for security and happiness. Some people are unwilling or emotionally unable to accept responsibility for their mistakes. When a mistake comes to light, they don't want to admit it was their fault. They fail to realize that the buck has to stop with them. Other immature people may be unable or unwilling to fulfill the trusts placed in them. They are *failure avoiders* rather than *success seekers.* They accept assignments but contribute little toward successful completion. The mature individual not only accepts the responsibility of carrying the ball down the field, but makes every effort to make the touchdown. And if he fails, he acknowledges his failure and tries to learn from his mistakes.

INDIVIDUALISM AND SELF-CONFIDENCE

The mature executive is aware of his capabilities, his goals, and the most effective ways to operate—in short, he knows where he is going. He has learned how to accept authority and organization constraints without being a conformist. He regards individual and interdependent contributions as essential to corporate success.

Mature executives welcome the participation of others. These executives surround themselves with employees who produce ideas, constantly confront challenge, and stimulate leadership. The immature leader seeks yes-men who will not remind him of his failings and inabilities. Strength in others is a threat only to the insecure. The mature executive who believes in himself and knows what he can deliver will carve his own path. He is a rebel with a cause, and he has learned how to cooperate with others in order to achieve contribution.

We all need to believe in ourselves and know what we can be counted on to accomplish and deliver. But we should cheerfully share credit with employees who help us and not constantly strive for the limelight and center stage.

PATIENCE

The mature executive has learned that for some problems there are no quick answers. He resists the temptation to seize the first solution that comes along. He is patient, but more than that he recognizes the value of having several alternatives. As a matter of operating procedure, former secretary of defense Robert McNamara insisted on options—three, four, or more courses of action. He was patient enough to wait for his subordinates to produce the options he demanded. Despite the political overtones that always surround a man in public office, those who knew him and his work say that he was a thinking administrator.

The impulse to master all aspects of any problem at once may interfere with effective problem solving. The immature would rather have the dime today than the quarter tomorrow. They have not learned to let time work for them. Because they are impatient to gain the perspective that time alone can give, they sometimes fail by making rash decisions.

An interesting anecdote is told of Abraham Lincoln, who often expressed his displeasure or anger with someone by dashing off a lengthy note to the individual outlining his grievances. Lincoln said it was a good device for letting off steam, but that he never sent the note until it had sat in his drawer for three days. Then if he still felt the same, he would send it. Not surprisingly, Lincoln never sent most of those notes. It was Lincoln's patience that enabled him to deal effectively with the problems of his day.

DECISION MAKING

Along with his patience in searching out alternative solutions, the mature executive is able to make a decision in the face of ambiguity. By weighing the facts, he recognizes the time when action must be taken—a time in fact when indecision amounts to a decision not to act. As Peter Drucker pointed out, "With regard to the future there can never be certainty, only possibilities." The mature executive has learned to accept this. He knows that if he waits for complete certainty he may miss the boat altogether. He is willing to take a calculated risk. Many management failures result not from a wrong decision but from no decision. *One can correct action but not inaction.*

SENSE OF HUMOR

Our sense of humor reveals our attitudes toward other people. The immature joke at the expense of others. They laugh when others are hurt or when someone else is made to look silly or inferior. Ethnic jokes are of this variety. Said George Bernard Shaw, "Some people would rather have their joke than their friend."

The mature executive knows that humor should be good-natured rather than demeaning or hostile. He uses humor to smooth the rough edges of human situations, as a lubricant to reduce interpersonal friction. The story is told of the irate politician who stormed into Lincoln's office and accused him of being two-faced. Lincoln, aware of his own homeliness, said, "I can assure you, sir, that if I had another face I would be wearing it."

The test of a person's sense of humor is his ability to laugh at himself. A top corporate executive was involved in an airline crash. While he was on the grass, dazed and bleeding, a reporter ran over and asked him if he had a statement for the press. The executive looked at the smoking ruins of the plane, looked at his own state of disarray, and found that the question tickled his own sense of the ridiculous. "Yes," he said, "fly American."

RESILIENCY

Life will always have its share of illness, pain, and disappointment. In *Effective Psychology for Managers*,[1] Mortimer Feinberg pointed out that the mature man bounces back from life's hurts with humor and resiliency. How does one react to the reality that pain must be borne and mistakes corrected? Do we pretend that all is well? Do we waste time agonizing over the past? Or do we view crushes as lessons from which we can learn?

The mature leader understands the value of resiliency and staying power. Setbacks do not destroy him because he views defeat as an improperly set objective or a poorly executed procedure. This sustaining power is the capacity to turn adversity into advantage. Sustaining power is not blind, unrealistic doggedness. It is the intelligent appraisal of failure, the capacity to learn from defeat in order to succeed another time.

From Shakespeare's *As You Like It* comes the story of a prince and his followers who were forced to leave their homeland and all that was dear to them. His followers grumbled and complained but were cheered by these few lines of counsel:

> Sweet are the uses of adversity,
> Which like the toad, ugly and venomous,
> Bears yet a precious jewel in its head.
> Thus our life, exempt from public haunts,
> Finds tongues in trees,
> Books in the running brooks,
> Sermons in stone,
> And good in everything.

[1] Englewood Cliffs, N.J.: Prentice-Hall, 1969.

The hero of the story was not a Pollyanna. Instead, he was trying to learn from adversity, to gain from failure, and he later returns to his homeland in triumph.

Such resiliency was exhibited by Abraham Lincoln, who suffered a number of serious defeats that would have deterred most men from ever trying again. He labored unsuccessfully as a shopkeeper and failed dismally in law practice. He failed in his race for the House of Representatives and he failed in his Senate race against Stephen A. Douglas. But he was elected to the presidency in 1860. The evidence of success in areas of human endeavor is all about us; the mature come back again and again until they win their objective.

TIME ORIENTATION

The mature individual does not live in the past. He lives and acts in the present. He *learns* from the past and *plans* for the future; he does not wait for his tomorrows. He follows the poet's advice to act in the living present.

We all know children who are going to be something when they grow up. Some adults have that same attitude. Some are middle-aged before they get that "lucky break" or when that "right opportunity" comes along. There are also some old people who have lived all their lives waiting for that golden tomorrow. As a character in one of Jean-Paul Sartre's plays said, "All my life I've been waiting for something to bite into, and now I find I have no teeth."

INTEGRATION

The mature man is integrated; that is, he does not fragment his life by verbalizing one way and behaving another way. Nor does he diffuse his energies by moving in ten different directions simultaneously. He is organized to handle multiple problems effectively, one at a time.

One of the marks of maturity is a person's ability to be honest with himself. The story of Lincoln walking four miles to return a penny to a woman who overpaid him when he was a store clerk is not just a nice story. It illustrates the character of a man who refused to be placed in a situation where his personal convictions would be compromised. There is a forthrightness, a self- and interpersonal honesty that binds the man together. The story is also told of Lincoln's campaign manager at the nominating convention trying to talk him into accepting a "deal" in exchange for convention delegates' votes. Lincoln's reply:

"I will make no bargains, nor will I be bound by any made in my behalf by others."

COMMUNICATION OF FEELING AND SENSITIVITY TOWARD OTHERS

Emotional maturity is the extent to which you can express your own feelings and convictions, balanced with consideration for the thoughts and feelings of others. It is indicated by one's ability to express and receive both negative and positive attitudes without feeling threatened. The mature man acknowledges that he has feelings; he is able to express love, disgust, anger. But he does so in a way that does not alienate others. There is a sense of craftsmanship in his work. He is committed to what he is doing; he is *enthusiastic* in the authentic sense of that word. (The word "enthusiasm" was coined by the Greeks to describe the early Christians. *En-theos* means the quality of having God or the spirit of God within.)

CONVICTIONS AND VALUES

The mature individual has a strong sense of values and an underlying philosophy that guides his behavior. He is not wishy-washy, but a human being with convictions. He can commit himself to an idea, a cause, or a principle. This explains the direction of purpose with which a mature executive makes and carries out decisions. He does not give up easily; he is willing to fight for what he believes. He is using a set of values that motivates his every action.

Immature individuals may be able to express their feelings intellectually, even elegantly, but when involved in conflict or controversy they fail to show consideration for others. They have not learned to be forthright without being caustic, impassioned without being abusive, firm without being cutting. The mature individual is able to disagree with but still respect the other person. He has the ability to let others express themselves. He is able to openly speak of problems and conflicts. The mature individual is at times an angry man, but this anger is his concern with a problem that goes beyond self-interest. A less effective person becomes angry because of his insecurity, directing his anger at others rather than at the problem.

ENTHUSIASM FOR WORK

An emotionally healthy supervisor knows how to enjoy his job. For the mature executive work is almost necessary for his survival as an individual. It is the way in which he communicates his self-image and reinforces his future.

The mature individual sees work not as drudgery but as creative expression. Erich Fromm realized that man has an inherent need to transcend the world about him and prove his mastery over his environment by changing it. Thus man has a need to create. When this creativity is frustrated, the alternative is to destroy. The mature individual is inquisitive, a creator and builder.

We have tried to briefly describe those characteristics we feel are inherent in mature managers. There is nothing mystical or magical about maturity. It is the ongoing and evolving result of a life that is focused, dedicated, and disciplined. We have described those whose total life experiences have brought them to the point where they can effectively utilize these qualities and who gain, as a matter of consequence, all that life has to offer. Few people have all the attributes that have been discussed, but the person who is making a conscious effort to develop these characteristics has found the key to maturity: the attitude of wanting to be all that one can become.

13

Ethics: The Vital Component

The manager is a person first, an executive second. Despite the emphasis on quantitative methods, rational processes, and improved systems design, the fact remains that at the moment of truth any man is left to function on his own resources. It is important, therefore, for any man in management to consider what his values are and how they affect his business decisions.

How does an individual make meaningful decisions in the continual context of ambiguity that modern society presents? How can business leaders and others make "right" decisions? What if the alternatives are not even known?

From Goethe's *Hermann und Dorothea* come these interesting and challenging lines:

> For in these unsettled times the man
> Whose mind is unsettled
> Only increases the evil and spreads it
> Wider and wider.
> While the man of firm purpose builds
> A world of his liking.

This chapter is adapted with permission from "Business Ethics: Analysis and Philosophy," *Personnel Journal*, April 1968.

A manager has a stewardship of power. Accompanying managerial power is the responsibility for ethics. There is a social impact of managerial decisions and behavior on people. Not only must a manager use his power to get results, and use his power along with other managers' power so that mutual results are gained, but when he puts on the mantle of managership he also needs to remind himself of the concomitant business ethics. Manager behavior inside and outside the company has ethical consequences that will reflect on a management career.

Management decisions have social values attached to them. A manager has the power to influence the very lives and well-being of people. Before a manager attempts to influence other people, to effect changes in them, he needs to clarify his own values. A manager must think through his philosophy of industrial living. He needs to consider some of his important values when making business decisions, because these decisions can have social consequences and consequences for the careers and even the mental health of other people. The man who does not appreciate the ethical ramifications of his business decisions tends to walk on thin ice because he develops the image, in other managers' eyes, of having little regard for anything other than himself and profits.

Leader behavior affects mental hygiene. Managers have the psychological welfare of many men in their hands. They can enhance the mental health of their people by appreciating the consequences of their behavior on those lives. Managers can build an employee's self-concept or they can easily cripple a subordinate's self-concept. The self-actualization, the self-realization, of men in organization life is in management's hands.

Many men have taken psychological punishment from managers who have been inept, who have not appreciated the consequences of their behavior on subordinates. Such managers may become notorious for their poor interpersonal relations. A manager in a major corporation was moved from supervising a major production unit to supervising a small research and development unit. The move made no sense, since the man was incompetent in research. Another manager who knew the situation said, "Look at it this way: Before, he was blighting the lives of sixty people. Now he can only blight the lives of six people."

Not only is there a social responsibility to subordinates but there is also an ethical responsibility to the customer—namely, the quality of the product. The manager is in a key position to influence the quality of the products that go to the customer; this is an ethical responsibility. Good business is ethical business.

He also has some customers inside—that is, his fellow managers. His social responsibility to these managers resides in the integrity of the information he gives them. High integrity of information is an ethical responsibility; one manager counts on another manager for quality information. False information is not funny.

While few would gainsay these sentiments, there is substantial question as to whether men in management really believe these high-sounding principles and, if they do, whether they are able to maintain their individual values in the midst of group-think.

A large percentage of today's college students report they do not want a career in business because there is a feeling among many young people that government or social work is where the action is. Somehow, they look outside business for meaningful and purposeful work, work that deals with the problems of the human situation. This disillusionment is a direct result of the equivocation and lack of moral leadership in business organizations. There seems to be a shrug-it-off attitude, a belief that ethics is a question that does not properly belong in the business world. Whenever one's values are relegated to a position of such minor emphasis, we are actively looking for trouble.

At the same time, business is being called upon to lead in new areas of responsibility that directly affect the national life and world peace. We must come to grips with some very difficult moral problems.

DEFINITION

What do we mean when we talk of ethics? Plato referred to ethics as a scientific investigation into the rightness or wrongness of decision making. Ethics concerns itself with two basic questions: What *is* and what *ought* to be? These questions define the difference between what is true, or the is, and what is right, or the ought. For example, it is true that price-fixing is a fact of business life in some industries. But the question of what ought to be is another matter.

Obviously, a person is incapable of making the right decision if he is uncertain of the issue, the truth, the "is" of reality. Before we attempt to make value judgments, it is necessary to deal with the reality of the situation. If we suspect an employee of pilferage and wrongly accuse him, we will have made an incorrect value judgment because we did not know the truth.

ISSUES

What are the ethical issues facing businessmen? What objective problems must be faced? The following are some of the problem areas.

Human utilization and development. High on the list of moral problems facing today's management is the unenlightened way in which people are used in industry. The waste of human resources, the stifling of creativity, and job-related neuroses are ample evidence that we are wrong in much of our practical dealings with people in the business world.

Truth in advertising. Before the passage of the Pure Food and Drug Act, a candy manufacturer advertised a candy guaranteed to make the user lose weight. The consumer was not told that inside each confection was a tapeworm segment. Is the advertising man justified in telling just the truth, and not the whole truth?

Price-fixing. The free enterprise system exerts constant pressure on price structures. Is the need for producing a stable segment of the economy for the benefit of companies, which in turn provide jobs and add to the national industrial strength, to be allowed precedence over the right of the consumer to buy in a free market?

Ecology. We have come forcefully face to face with the damaging impact management decisions can have on the planet. Spaceship earth is badly in need of some clearer definitions of the needs of man.

Any business question. There can be no limited area of discussion when we speak of ethics. We can't first consider, "What business decisions do we want to make?" and then walk to the other side of the table and say, "What ethical decisions do we want to make?" The two are inseparable; the moral element is implicit in every situation.

This list is short and abstract, and no doubt most of us would like to keep it that way. The ethical businessman constantly lengthens the list and defines the issues.

APPLIED STANDARDS

Any discussion about values implies the existence of standards against which alternatives are measured. These standards can be subsumed under the following headings.

The subjective standard. Morality is viewed as nothing more than a personal judgment on the part of each individual. If others are similar to ourselves, we are likely to consider them moral. If their patterns of action and beliefs are sufficiently different from ours it is probable that we would consider them ethically unsound. This somewhat egotistical view, which fractionates society, is the standard most often applied.

The normative standard. Morality is that standard approved by the greatest number of people. Those who differ from group norms are punished. This is the voice of society, the culture, the group. Legal standards are but the norms of a past society.

Behavior and thought patterns acceptable in one time and place may not be so in another setting. Concerning homosexuality, the Old Testament says: "If a man also lieth down with a man as he lieth with a woman, both of them have committed an abomination. They shall verily be put to death. Their blood shall be upon them." However, in ancient Greece, sexual relationships among members of the same sex were encouraged. Said Plato, in speaking of homosexuals: "They act in this way because they have a strong soul, manly courage, and a virile character."

The normative standard is more stable than the subjective, but it is not permanently so, as witness the "new morality."

The objective standard. Morality, as dictated by religious beliefs, is claimed to be objective, in that it does not change over time and is true for all men. Our society, legal system, and traditions are inseparably bound to the Judeo-Christian ethic. One problem that must be reconciled by those who accept this absolutist position is the large number of creeds. As Mark Twain said, "Man's the only creature with the true religion—several of them."

A second objective standard is posited by the existential psychologists, who see the fully functioning, self-actualized person as the standard of measurement. Their argument has some merit, but very little supportive data.

Aristotle once said, "Thought alone moves nothing." A standard is not just a talking point, but a tool for action. Which standard do we choose? It has been our observation that most people are rather eclectic and at any given moment in time they take from sets of values those standards that best fit the situation. This hippety-hoppety rabbit habit of never really picking a standard is termed "situation ethics." This constant changing, with no maintenance of consistency with self, reminds one of the chameleon that changed color every time the environment changed. One day, while crossing a patchwork quilt, the effort proved fatal.

PEOPLE RESOURCES

Harry Stack Sullivan coined the term "significant others" to describe those persons who have a major influence in our lives. To whom does the businessman turn when faced with an ethical dilemma?

Business associates. The data indicate that a man will seek cues from his superiors, but rarely ask for advice from his peers and never from subordinates.

Family. The wife may serve as an emotional sponge, but is usually not asked for an opinion. Either the male sees it as a threat to his masculinity or does not value her opinion in business matters.

Friends. No data available, but probably not a resource.

Clergyman. Although the clergyman is perhaps one of the experts on ethical matters, the overwhelming majority of businessmen do not ask for his advice. He is considered unqualified to speak on business matters.

Industrial psychologist. One of the most significant developments in this area is the increasing use of the psychologist as a resource, even though he may be unqualified in the businessman's area of endeavor.

Why does the businessman seek counsel? Apparently for three reasons: He wants support for his views; he wants a sounding board with neither support nor rejection of his views; he wants his hands slapped for a wrong he is about to do.

AREAS OF RESPONSIBILITY

The businessman is responsible to many different groups of people. He must satisfy the demands of each group and continually balance his actions in reference to them. In short, he does not act in a vacuum but in relation to others. Those to whom the businessman is responsible include self, family, employees, management, subordinates, stockholders, customers, creditors, government, society, and world.

Conceivably individual circumstances would determine the priority given each group. Data indicate, however, that top executives give highest priority to stockholders. No other group was even a close second. Responsibility to society ranked at the very bottom. Such disturbing findings probably have to be interpreted in light of today's concept of the purpose of business. Most businessmen still cling to the nineteenth century concept that the sole objective of business is to make a profit. They have not yet grasped the significant fact that in twentieth century America, the objective of business has to be the proper utilization of resources for the benefit of others. A profit is still a necessary part of the total picture, but it is not the primary purpose. Any businessman who forgets that fact for very long is asking for government intervention.

PERSONAL INVENTORY

Ethical judgments are usually clouded by the intrusion of personal biases. Decisions based on irrational fears, prejudices, likes, or preferences are made daily. It is pathetic to see a businessman who can quote facts and figures on any aspect of his business, yet who has not made an evaluation of himself.

What are your beliefs, your goals, your biases, your prejudices? What makes you happy or unhappy? What gives purpose to your life? Do you think others are basically good or basically evil? What is your self-image? What thought processes do you use? Do you know your strengths and weaknesses?

Have you made such an inventory a regular part of your life? Are you constantly aware of the subjective stamp you place on decisions? Do you know when such subjectivity is needed? Do you feel confident in your judgment? Do you have a valid reason to feel confident? Most important, after gaining accurate self-knowledge, do you sincerely try to make your decision making more ethical?

INVOLVEMENT LEVEL

Our degree of involvement influences our decision making. The man who views with abhorrence the idea of killing another man in hand-to-hand combat, yet can go to work and sit at a console waiting for an order to "push the button," is too distant from the consequences of his actions to sense the ethical paradox. This detachment also plagues the businessman, who is often removed from the effects of his work. The ability to project oneself into the situation is what is needed.

POWER

The higher a man rises in the corporate structure the greater will be his formal authority and power to act. This is needed because the ethical problems will also be greater. There is a tendency in any bureaucracy to evade responsibility by bucking the problem upward. This was the defense strategy at the Nuremberg trials. But it should be stressed that this argument—that a man is not responsible simply because his manager has more power than he—is not particularly acceptable.

The factors discussed above are all operative in ethical dilemmas. They are not the only factors, but they are sufficient to demonstrate the need for an organized analysis of ethical problems. Because there are so many variables operating, it becomes imperative to isolate as many factors as possible. A step-by-step approach to some of the ethical problems facing today's business world is badly needed.

THEORIES ON MORALITY AND ETHICS

Other, broader and deeper questions are concerned with the philosophical implications of some difficult ethical questions. In questioning our ability to make "right" decisions, we have involved ourselves in several conflicting systems of thought. The issues raised have to do with knowledge theory and man's view of himself.

Moral Relativism Versus
Moral Absolutism

How can a man choose a meaningful standard by which to judge his actions and the actions of others? The issue that most of us are battling is deciding where we stand in relation to our personal moral and ethical convictions.

If you have some religious convictions, you probably feel quite strongly about the eternal nature of values. This is a moral-absolutist position. Moral relativists, on the other hand, may be torn by the pressures of day-to-day decisions that seemingly make it necessary to compromise personal beliefs for the sake of pleasing the boss or selling a contract. Some relativists may be convinced that it is always best to lean the way the wind blows. Your commitment to such a way of life may be openly cynical or it may be intellectually honest.

If there are no objective, permanent, and absolute standards, then it is ridiculous to speak of making right or wrong decisions in the context of time. Today's right answer will be tomorrow's wrong answer. This is where moral absolutists have an easier time. All one has to do is discover the standard and cling to it. Time or God will prove that you have acted correctly.

The moral relativists assert that a standard is just a group consensus or individual desire. While this idea allows more comfort for the individual as compared to the absolutist position, it becomes very easy to get sloppy in one's thinking.

Determinism Versus Free Will

In all this talk about man's choosing and the decision-making process, we have been assuming that man is free to make choices and that he wills decisions. Suppose that assumption is false. It is obviously meaningless to talk of choosing if man is not free to choose.

There is a large body of evidence that would seem to indicate that a strict determinism is operative everywhere in the known universe. A strict cause-and-effect relationship governs everything from the movement of planets to skin color in humans. This is the basis of all science. Physics was the first branch of science to demonstrate that if A happened, then B must result. Charles Darwin extended the theory from the inanimate to life forms, both plant and animal. He suggested an elaborate chain of causation that eventually produced the human species.

Psychology then took over in applying the implications. In 1904, Ivan Pavlov received a Nobel prize for his work in discovering the conditioned reflex. He rang a bell and at the same time gave a piece of meat to his pet dog. Soon, after the process was repeated for a certain number of trials, the dog would salivate when the bell rang even though no meat was presented. This disarmingly simple laboratory procedure demonstrated that behavior could be shaped and controlled.

Sigmund Freud came to the same conclusion by observing the great influence that childhood experiences had in later life. A picture was emerging that man was not free: Each individual did not wholly shape his own life, as others were responsible for his development. The sociologists picked up the argument and proclaimed that man was the product of his environment. People holding this deterministic view felt that since man was not free from his environment—since he had been shaped by it—he was not responsible for his actions.

Free-will advocates have no evidence to refute the claim except to doggedly insist that they do make choices. The determinists answer that we have only an illusion of choice. In other words, a determinist would say that a businessman's decisions are completely determined by factors in his background.

The problem with such a philosophy is that it is nihilistic. Man's life can have no purpose or meaning in such a philosophy, and any business action would be justified. In this context, one can't help but think of some of the decisions made by industrial corporations in Nazi Germany.

The Existential Hypothesis

During the past 50 years, there has emerged what purports to be an alternative to the dilemma of determinism. Existentialism is concerned with the actual realities of existence more than with theories that result in indecision and inaction. Although it has great implication for religious faith, it is not primarily religious in its orientation.

Existentialism concerns itself with phenomenology, that is, that which can be known through experience rather than through logical or reasoned processes. What is it that I as an individual know for sure? I seem to know these things about my existence:

That I am. In the Old Testament before God revealed his name he was asked what it was. God said, "I am that I am." There isn't anything more profound that can be said about a person than that he is and exists.

That death comes to all. I am not a member of the Pepsi generation, nor do I live my life on bubbles and illusions. When President John Kennedy and Martin Luther King, Jr., were assassinated there was a universal shock as people comprehended the reality of death. I am aware of my finality.

That there are ultimate questions. There are many questions that I can ask; there are only a few worth asking. What is the purpose of my life? What about death? I live in a world where there are more questions than answers, where uncertainty abounds.

That I am free. I am not free to do everything, but free to do some things. I am a determinant in a universe that does function on a basis of causal relationships.

That I am responsible. Freedom necessitates responsibility. I cannot blame others or excuse myself because to do so would deny that *I am.*

That life calls for commitment. My existence, if it is to be meaningful, means that I must meet life and embrace it. As Robert Kennedy said about his brother, "If there is a lesson from his life and from his death, it is that in this world of ours none of us can afford to be lookers-on, the critics standing on the sidelines."

That faith is the operating basis for life. The only way to know that life has meaning is to give myself to it. I can never know until then the truth of the proposition. Sören Kierkegaard called it the leap into the abyss.

That mankind is my concern. Man's welfare is my ultimate concern because I affirm about him all that I affirm about myself. It does matter how I act toward others.

This existential point of view goes against those who want to opt out of life. A denial of selfhood, a running away from being, characterizes too much of our society and the business world.

Business has been called on to lead in many areas to which businessmen have not customarily given much consideration. Illiteracy, starvation, and other basic human problems are outstripping our ability to cope with them. According to the World Health Organization, 20,000 people starve to death daily. It is doubtful that a world so unbalanced can long endure. This marble game is for keeps.

But business leaders, by and large, have failed to exercise leadership. They have failed to provide new ideas or even to commit themselves to the search for new ideas. There has been an unwillingness to accept this challenge which could well mean the difference between continued success or failure for our society. This is due not only to a lack of corporate leadership but also to the failure of individuals within the corporate structure to overcome their own inertia. General Omar N. Bradley too accurately referred to us as ethical infants and moral adolescents. It does not need to be that way.

On that eventful Christmas Eve in Dickens' *Christmas Carol,* when Scrooge relives his past and sees his future, he is visited by his long-dead business partner, Jacob Marley, who wears about his neck the chains he has forged for himself link by link and yard by yard. He is so morose that Scrooge tries to cheer him by saying, "You were always a good man in business, Jacob." Marley's classic reply is relevant to us and to our time:

Business! Mankind was my business; charity, mercy, forbearance, and benevolence were all my business. The dealings of my trade were but a drop of water in the vast comprehensive ocean of my business.